BY RICHARD M. LANGWORTH AND
THE EDITORS OF CONSUMER GUIDE®

HI-PERFORMANCE CHEVROLET

Contents

Introduction 4

Louis Weber, President
Publications International, Ltd.
3841 West Oakton Street
Skokie, Illinois 60076

Library of Congress Catalog Card Number: 81-82875
ISBN: 0-88365-591-8

Photo Credits:
William Bailey, Terry Boyce, The Pat Chappell Collection, Chevrolet Motor Division, Edelbrock Automotive Performance Products, David Gooley, Phil Hall, Holley Carburetors, Bud Juneau, Richard M. Langworth, Jan P. Norbye, Gregory Wells.

Introduction

Thirty years ago only the most fanatical Chevy enthusiast would have dreamed of what was to come from America's favorite automaker. Back in 1951, the Chevrolet line comprised four nearly identical series of very nice-looking, well-finished, soundly built . . . utterly dull automobiles. There was only one engine: a solid, stolid six. It came with a three-speed column stick, and you could order optional overdrive or Powerglide automatic. You could also have a radio, a heater, and a set of whitewall tires—which just about completed the accessories list.

Just five years later, Chevrolet's tradition of making reliable, if boring, basic transport for the masses would be totally eclipsed by a dramatically different product: Harley Earl's brilliant all-new design for 1955, coupled with Ed Cole's superb small-block 265 V-8. Both these works are recognized today as auto industry benchmarks. And just three years' worth of Chevys, the now-revered 1955–57 models, have become perhaps the most popular—certainly the most numerous—collector cars of the period. They were so successful in their time that, today, children of those who bought them new are collecting them, even driving them daily. And why not? There's nothing wrong with paying $10,000 for a nice '55 Nomad that will likely be worth $15,000 in 1985 instead of spending the same amount for a brand-new Caprice that isn't half as interesting.

The story of Chevrolet performance begins with the Corvette, introduced in 1953. The new V-8 was, of course, still on the drawing boards at that time, so Chevrolet had to settle for a modified version of its basic six for its fiberglass-bodied sports car. But that first Corvette, with its Powerglide transmission, whitewall tires, and wraparound windshield, was the all-important first step in altering Chevy's time-worn image—and in directly challenging Ford for the hearts of the high-performance customer in the low-price field.

Panned and derided by the *cognoscenti* of the sports-car world, the early Corvette managed to scrape through. Sales of the '55 models were hardly worth mentioning, but something else was. The V-8 had arrived, and gave Corvette the performance it justly deserved—and badly needed. Likewise, the soon-to-be legendary 265 worked its powerful magic on Chevy's passenger cars, with their deft styling and memorable models like the Bel Air hardtops and convertibles and the unique Nomad wagon. Chevy's course had now been charted for the years ahead.

Why did truly fast, roadworthy Chevys appear so suddenly, virtually overnight? Was it really necessary to change a top-selling car line so drastically? Couldn't Chevrolet have simply gone on building nothing but six-cylinder family cars? The answers lie in the transformation of the American auto market after World War II.

Automotive development had largely passed through the initial "experimental" period by 1930. The industry had pretty much settled on front-mounted, gasoline-powered engines, rear-wheel drive, and closed bodies. But when the Depression hit, there wasn't enough money or customers around to encourage large-scale production of specialty or performance cars. Of course, fast cars did exist—notably, the custom-bodied classics by such prestigious makers as Packard, Stutz, Cadillac, and Duesenberg—but these were quite rare, reserved by price for those fortunate few who had managed to hold onto their money after the Great Crash. The rest of the public went on driving inexpensive Fords, Chevys, and Plymouths—whenever they could buy gasoline, that is.

World War II changed all that. It put a quick end to the Depression, and ushered in a quarter-century of prosperity that has, in relative terms, yet to be equalled. It was this prosperity that led to our widespread fascination with foreign sports cars. Americans had never heard of an MG or Jaguar before GIs began spending some of their accumulated back pay and bringing them home. The idea of a hot rod—an old roadster body packing a souped-up engine for extra power—captured the imagination of younger enthusiasts in the early postwar years, though some "rods" had been built earlier. Likewise, the customizing craze started sweeping the country around 1950. When engine technology resulted in a new generation of high-compression overhead-valve V8s in the late '40s, the horsepower race was underway. Americans began to buy "hot" cars in unheard of numbers, because so many at last had the money to indulge their pent-up passion for performance. Soon, speed and styling became the overriding design concerns of Detroit manufacturers.

Until the mid-1950s, though, most people spelled performance F-O-R-D. Henry and Edsel Ford's decision to one-up Chevrolet with a low-priced V-8 in 1932 had made Ford the first—and sometimes the only—choice for performance-minded buyers of moderate means. Terraplanes, Chryslers, and certain Studebakers were fine performers, but they were peripheral to the perennial Ford/Chevy sales race because they cost far more. With Chevy sticking to its six and Plymouth waiting until 1933 to go from four to

"The Hot One" that started it all: the brilliant 1955 Chevrolet,
selected to pace that year's Indy 500

six cylinders, the low-price "high-performance" market was strictly Ford country.

After the war, Ford, with help from Mercury, continued to dominate "performance car" sales. Wealthier buyers soon had the choice of modern ohv V-8s from Cadillac, Oldsmobile, and Chrysler, and Studebaker started producing a fine small-block for 1951. By the time Ed Cole arrived at Chevy Division, performance was crucial to sales success. This meant that Chevy would have to have a V-8 as soon as possible.

The answer to our question, then, is that the Division could not have remained successful with the kind of car it was building in 1951. The advent of Chevy performance in the mid-'50s was thus inevitable, at least from a commercial standpoint.

The V-8 engine certainly saved the Corvette, which was going nowhere until it was offered. Likewise, it played an important role in Chevy's passenger cars. By 1957, you could order one with an engine that produced an incredible one horsepower per cubic inch. For 1962, there was even a rear-engine Corvair that wrung 150 horsepower from 145 cubic inches.

The first half of this book reviews the watershed developments in Chevrolet's performance history. The second half, beginning with Chapter VII, tells what happened after Chevy had firmly established itself in the performance stakes. These are two distinct phases. Before 1960, the hotter Chevys were designed around smallish engines that in no way were meant to rival a Chrysler hemi or an Oldsmobile Rocket for all-out power. After that, Chevy began to compete directly with the "big" cars not only in power but also in engine and vehicle size. The big-inch Impala Super Sports of the early '60s could, in many cases, leave the hottest Chrysler or Oldsmobile far behind.

The SS Chevys of the '60s came about in part because of a basic reorientation in people's attitudes about cars. Before about 1958, it was taken for granted that a Chevrolet should be smaller and less powerful than a Cadillac, or even an Olds. But by the mid-'50s, "longer-lower-and-wider" was as important as performance to sales success. Soon, the "low-price

three," including Chevy, had ballooned until they were nearly as large as the big luxury makes in most dimensions.

The appearance of these much larger Chevys (and Fords and Plymouths, too) was arguably not for the best. As part of a generation of grossly overweight, fuel-guzzling cars, they resulted from market forces that flew in the face of what we would later recognize (almost too late) as a finite supply of petroleum. Only after gasoline shortages caused by the Arab oil embargo of 1973–74 and the rapid rise in imported oil prices in the late '70s did Detroit begin moving in the opposite direction. But the freewheeling, free-spending spirit of the '50s and '60s also led to the fabulous fuel-injected 283 and monster big-block engines like the 409 and 396. And while fuel was plentiful and cheap, it also produced some of the most exciting cars ever seen on American roads.

Looking back—which is one of the more pleasant things car buffs can do these days—it might seem as if there was no real reason for Chevy to build anything remotely like an Impala SS409. But some of the best things in life are born not of logic, but of a zest for living. And who can begrudge us a little nostalgia—if only as a short break from our diet of 85-mph speedometers, $1.40-a-gallon gas, and 0–60 mph in 20 seconds? Fortunately, many performance Chevys still survive. More and more of them are being rescued from the junkyard, because the ultimate truth about all older cars has now sunk in with iron reality: there won't be any more like them—ever.

If that sounds gloomy, take heart. There will still be performance cars from Chevy in the years ahead, though they will certainly be more "European" in character, for the era of the big brutes is certainly past. Yet everyone who today drives a Corvette Sting Ray or an early Z-28 Camaro or a "fuelie" '57 has preserved that time for us all. They are driving retired champs, fully deserving of the same praise and adulation as a Joe Dimaggio or a Rocky Marciano. To the cars, the men and women who built them, and the enthusiasts who have lovingly preserved them, this book is dedicated. Let there be no mistake: we remember.

The quartet of Corvette show cars displayed at the 1954 Motorama (from top): Nomad wagon, "Corvair" fastback, hardtop prototype, and the production '54 roadster.

1953-55 Corvette:

First of the Performance Chevys

There's no doubt that the Corvette was the first of the performance Chevys. And in recent years, there have been those who thought it might be the last. Times are improving for the automobile industry, though, and there are quite a few exciting developments coming from Chevrolet in the 1980s. Corvette will certainly continue to be among the quickest cars in the Chevy line, just as it has been ever since June 30th of 1953 when the first one rolled out of the Flint assembly plant.

There wasn't much to work with for the first Corvette. The decision to build a sports car, at least as a showpiece for the Motorama, was taken in 1952. Newly appointed Chevrolet Engineering director Edward N. Cole had not yet begun to shake his staff by its collective scruff, and time was short. And if most of the car's mechanical pieces would have to be taken from Chevy's parts shelf, they hardly promised excitement. This included the tried and true—but ordinary and slow—"Blue Flame Six."

None of this daunted Harley Earl, longtime chief of GM's Art & Colour Studio, that hotbed of automotive design from the 1930s right on through to the '60s. Earl had watched with intense interest as companies like Glasspar had developed glass-reinforced plastic (GRP) into a reliable material for car bodies. Also, he personally liked (and had driven) a lot of low-slung two-seaters. In 1952, he had built a fiberglass version of a standard Chevy convertible. He liked what he saw, and commissioned the plastic two-seat roadster that was to emerge in mid-1953 as the first Corvette.

The Corvette's styling expressed contemporary themes favored by the Art & Colour staff: wraparound windshield, pushbutton door handles, nerf-type bumpers, metal top cover. Chrome-plated stone guards were used as much to protect the sunken headlamps as to add flavor to the front end. The toothy grille was a natural for the '50s, and later became the darling of customizers, who stuck it onto everything from big Chevys to Kaisers. Clean-lined and ground-hugging, the Corvette had the "wasp-waist" look that fascinated Earl in those years, its beltline dipping aft of the doors before rolling back toward pointed taillamps and a rounded rear end.

The styling job was completed in remarkably short order. The slim lead time, however, combined with budgetary considerations to make use of production components a must. Young Bob McLean laid out the chassis, starting, unnaturally, from the rear. He placed the seats ahead of a stock Chevy rear axle, then moved the engine and transmission as far back as possible to improve weight distribution, aiming for a 50/50 split front to rear. The drivetrain was also lowered for a lower center of gravity. Wheelbase was pegged at 102 inches, apparently because this was the same length as that of the Jaguar XK-120, one of Earl's "benchmark" cars.

Predictably, power was supplied by the 235 cubic-inch "Blue Flame" engine, then delivering 105 horsepower. For the Corvette, it was modified by a high-lift long-duration cam, hydraulic valve lifters, and a high-compression head, all of which brought power up considerably. Triple Carter type YH sidedraft carbs mounted on a special aluminum manifold did the rest. Result: 150 bhp at 4500 rpm. Chevy didn't have a manual transmission at the time suitable for an engine of this power, so engineers substituted two-speed Powerglide automatic, with revised shift points for more sporting response.

The suspension was of Chevy design and boringly conventional, but spring rates, shock settings, and ride stabilizer were all recalibrated to suit the Corvette.

Corvette prototype at its Waldorf debut, 1953

An early production 1953 Corvette

1954 Corvette

finished in Polo White, with red and white interiors and black tops. All were equipped with 6.70 × 15 whitewall tires, Delco signal-seeking radio, and recirculating hot-water heater. The instrument panel included a clock and a 5000-rpm tachometer.

Rare and desirable today, the 1953 'Vette was considered something less than wonderful when new. Its typical 0–60 mph time was 11 seconds, and top speed was about 105 mph—not bad for 1953, but hardly in keeping with the state of the sports-car art even then. But its significance in the Chevy performance story—aside from being the first of the breed—is that it demonstrated the Division's new interest in sporting machinery, with the promise of more and better things to come.

Few significant changes were made to the Corvette for 1954, but running alterations took place through the model year. The '54s had tan (instead of black) tops and top irons, and gas and brake lines were relocated inboard of the righthand main frame rail. The engine carried a new-style rocker arm cover, the wiring harness was cleaned up, and more plastic-insulated wire replaced the fabric variety. Engines, built at Flint, were suffixed "F54YG." This was also the first year when a choice of colors became available

Likewise, the Saginaw steering was a stock GM component, but had a much quicker 16:1 ratio. And the Corvette's steering wheel was an inch smaller in diameter than that of Chevy passenger cars.

The 300 Corvettes built in the 1953 model year were essentially handmade pilot units. As such, they showed a considerable amount of improvisation. The first 25, for example, used stock Bel Air wheel covers. To simplify assembly and parts inventory, all '53s were

The Enthusiast Engineer

No Chevrolet story is complete without a few words on Ed Cole, the dynamo who came to manage the Division in 1953. It was Cole who almost single-handedly changed Chevy's image overnight.

Born on a farm in Marne, Michigan in 1909, Ed had always been interested in things mechanical. He tinkered with tractors, radios, cars, and trucks. Entering the GM Institute, Cole took part in a work-study program affiliated with Cadillac, and in 1933 was hired by that Division as a full-time engineer. Before and during World War II, he designed Army light tanks, combat vehicles, and a new engine for the M-3 tank.

Following the war, Cole temporarily involved himself with rear-engine prototypes as possibilities for both Chevrolet and Cadillac at that time. Soon, he was concentrating on engine work with Cadillac's John Gordon, and together they came up with the significant short-stroke Cadillac V-8 of 1949. This superb new overhead-valve engine was 220 pounds lighter, seven percent more powerful, and 10 percent more economical than the old L-head V-8 it replaced. Following a 30-month spell as manager of the Cadillac Cleveland plant, he came to Chevrolet.

"Chevy," Cole once said, "was an outfit you couldn't get your arms around." He became chief engineer in April 1952, and immediately enlarged the engineering staff from 850 to 2900. With this team he forged the milestone 265 V-8, followed by the legendary 283. He became Division general manager in July 1956, and was elected a GM vice-president.

In November 1961, after having played a major role in development of the Corvair, Cole was appointed group executive, Car and Truck Division, and elected to the GM board of directors. In July 1965, he was elected executive vice-president in charge of staff operations. On October 30, 1967, he reached the top rung of the tall GM ladder, being elected president and chief operating officer of the corporation.

After having sparked the catalytic converter project, the multi-million-dollar downsizing of the GM line for the late '70s, and the Wankel engine (ultimately mothballed, which was a disappointment to him), Cole retired from GM on September 30, 1974. He couldn't get cars out of his blood, however, and joined Checker Motors in Kalamazoo. He was working on various advanced engineering projects, including a new engine that could run on a fuel derived from air and water, when he died in a crash of his private aircraft in May 1977.

The industry trade weekly, Automotive News, perhaps best described Cole in its obituary. He was "an auto man, first, last, and all the time. He knew his industry as few men know it. He loved it as few have loved it. . . . He touched off a spark with anyone who came in contact with him, and that spark will be remembered for a long time."

(approximate percentages noted in parentheses): Pennant Blue metallic (16) with tan interior, Sportsman Red (4) with red and white interior, and the usual Polo White (80) with red interior. A very small number, as few as six, were painted black, and also carried the red interior. Model year production was 3640 units. For 1954, right on up through 1981, the cars were built in St. Louis, Missouri.

Sales for 1954 proved disappointing. Even though Corvette was now available in reasonable quantities from dealers, public response was mixed. Some analysts thought prospective buyers might have viewed it as neither fish nor fowl—not a true "road and track" machine, but not a genuine tourer, either. Purists objected to the automatic transmission and such non-functional items as simulated knock-off wheels. Sporting pleasure drivers didn't like the rude side curtains and manual folding top, and preferred fresh-air heaters to the recirculating unit. There were some service problems, too, water leaks in particular. Sales fell soon after the '54s were introduced, and production ground to a halt, with 1500 units left unsold at the end of the model year. That's an amazing fact in light of the popularity the 'Vette would soon achieve.

Harley Earl had proposed a mild facelift for 1955 involving a new, wider eggcrate grille similar to that of the '55 Chevrolet. Budget limitations prevented this, however, so Corvette remained much as it had been before—with one big exception. This was the new 265-cid V-8 engine. It was ostensibly an option, but actually no more than 10 six-cylinder Corvettes were built for the whole model year. Here at last was the real get-up-and-go Chevrolet's sports car needed.

Though the Corvette's V-8 shared its basic design with the engine used in the passenger-car line (see Chapter II for engineering details), it developed more horsepower: 195 at 5000 rpm. The performance gain it offered over the six was fantastic, with 0–60 mph coming up in 8.5–9.0 seconds and top speed approaching 120 mph. The V-8 Corvette was substantially quicker than most passenger cars of 1955. Perhaps more important, it was quicker than Ford's Thunderbird. Chevrolet took heart in that.

Color choices shifted in 1955, with Harvest Gold replacing Pennant Blue early in the model year. Corvette Copper, a sharp metallic, was also made available, and Gypsy Red replaced Sportsman Red. Bodies were smoother and thinner in section than before, and workmanship was better. The V-8 models carried an automatic choke for the first time in production and a new 12-volt electrical system (curiously the few sixes built used a 6-volt one). Powerglide was retained, similar in specification to the 1953–54 unit. However, its vacuum modulator feature was dropped in keeping with all 1955 Chevrolet production, so that kickdown was now governed solely by speed and throttle position. Late in the model year, a three-speed manual transmission was offered with close-ratio gearing. On cars so equipped the rear axle ratio was shortened to 3.70:1 from the Powerglide model's 3.55:1.

Saleswise, 1955 again proved disappointing. Production was only 700 units, a mere fraction of the 16,000-plus Thunderbirds Ford was selling. But the decision to continue and improve the Corvette had already been made. The all-new 1956 model was in the works, and would turn out to be one of the most exciting performance Chevys of all time. With the 1955 Corvette, Chevrolet reached the jumping off place in its quest for sports-car performance. It now had a terrific V-8 and a manual transmission. All that was left was to give the car dramatic styling. And that was soon accomplished, as we shall see in Chapter IV.

Large "V" in "Chevrolet" fender script identified new 265 V-8. Almost all '55 Corvettes had it.

Milestone Engines/I:

265, 283, and 348 V-8s

Shortly after Ed Cole took over as Chevrolet chief engineer, GM board chairman Alfred P. Sloan asked him about his plans for the department. Although they included tripling the engineering staff, Sloan just waved him on. Quipped then-GM president Charles Wilson to Cole, "I'll bet that's the first time you ever had your plans approved without submitting them."

To alter Chevrolet's time-honored image from builder of mundane people-movers to performance-car specialist, Cole knew he would need a V-8 engine. His predecessor, Ed Kelley, had toyed with a V-6 and a 231 cubic-inch V-8, both of which Cole rejected. But he didn't have much time to consider alternatives. When all the development phases were accounted for, there would be just 15 weeks in which to design a new powerplant for the 1955 model line. With the help of Kelley and motor engineer Harry Barr, Cole made it.

The 265-cid V-8 of 1955

"I had worked on V-8 engines all my professional life," Cole said later. "I had lived and breathed engines. Barr and I were always saying how we would do it if we could ever design a new engine. You just *know* you want five main bearings—there's no decision to make. We knew that a certain bore/stroke relationship was the most compact. We knew we'd like a displacement of 265 cubic inches, and that automatically established the bore and stroke. And we never changed any of this. We released our engine for tooling direct from the drawing boards—that's how crazy and confident we were."

Of course, even a ground-up engine had to be designed within certain parameters. Since it was intended for Chevrolet, the new V-8 had to be relatively inexpensive to build and efficient in operation. It need not be a poor engine—and it was anything but—yet it had to be a model of simplicity and production economics, which it was.

One of the outstanding features that made the 265 such a watershed development was the lack of a common rocker shaft. Each rocker arm was entirely independent of the others, so that deflection of one had no effect on the others. Each was assembled over a valve stem and pushrod, retained by a fulcrum ball and lock nut. Regardless of whether mechanical or hydraulic valve lifters were used, the valves were lashed by turning the lock nut. In addition, this arrangement reduced reciprocating weight, which allowed higher rpm and cut down on raw materials. The intake manifold provided a common water outlet to both heads. The heads were die-cast with integral valve guides, and were completely interchangeable. The valvetrain design was shared with that year's slightly larger Pontiac V-8, which was designed along the same lines.

A short stroke meant short connecting rods—just 5.7 inches center distance for a stroke ratio of 1.9. Pressed-in piston pins eliminated the slitting of the rod and the need for a locking bolt. Five main bearings of equal diameter carried maximum loads in their lower halves. "By reducing the maximum oil film loads through omission of the oil groove in the lower half," noted the *SAE Journal,* "the capacity of the main bearings is increased approximately 100 percent, and wear is reduced." More weight was saved by circulating the oil through hollow pushrods, providing

Ed Cole (left) is credited with much of the 265 V-8 design. It made the 1955 Bel Air hardtop one of "The Hot Ones."

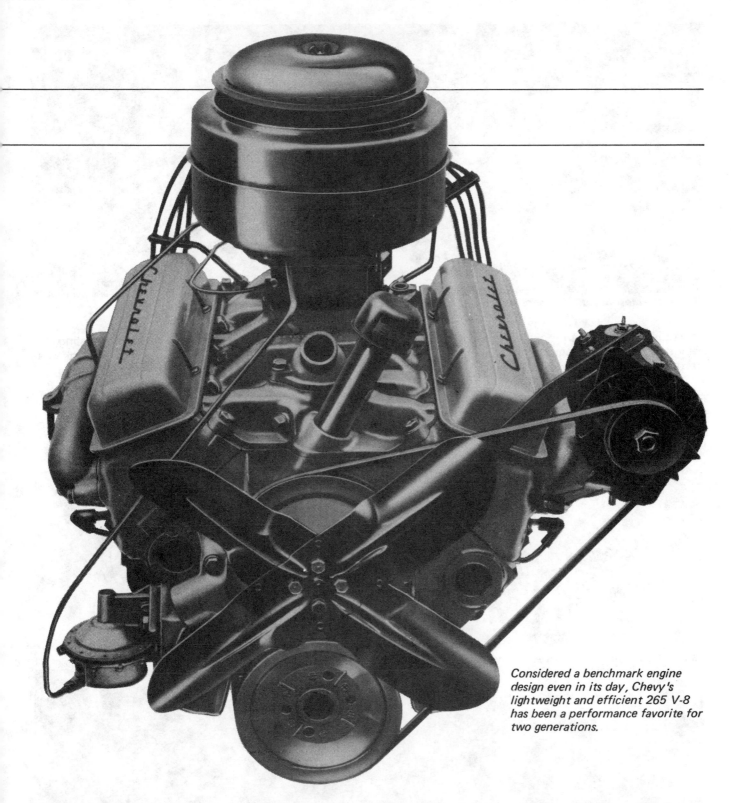

Considered a benchmark engine design even in its day, Chevy's lightweight and efficient 265 V-8 has been a performance favorite for two generations.

splash lube to the rockers and valve stems. This meant that separate and costly oil feeder lines were unnecessary.

Further details included "autothermic" pistons with three rings, slipper-type aluminum units with a circumferential expander for the single oil ring providing axial and radial force to control oil burning. Instead of alloy iron, the crankshaft was made of pressed forged steel because of its higher specific gravity and modulus of elasticity. Newly developed forging processes allowed Chevrolet to reduce overall crank length. A chart of torsional vibration showed very

One of the most beautiful wagons ever, the V-8 1955 Nomad was also one of the quickest.

low peaks without sharp points throughout most of the range; adding a harmonic balancer eliminated remaining torsional vibration.

The exhaust manifolds were routed near the top of the cylinder heads, with exhaust passages pointing upward and out, and the entire length of the ports was water-jacketed. "This minimizes the transfer of distortion loads back to the valve seats," the *Journal*

New V-8 and optional four-speed transmission made the redesigned 1956 Corvette a sports car to be reckoned with.

The big news for '57 was the fuel-injected 283. "Fuelie" 'Vettes are prime collector cars today.

noted, "and dissipates heat uniformly from the valve area." Chevy switched to a 12-volt electrical system for the 265 that provided more efficient generator output, better starter-motor operation, and adequate voltage for the powerplant's higher compression.

Because the new engine had better heat rejection properties than the "Blue Flame Six," a smaller radiator could be used, which reduced rate and frontal radiator area. Overall, the V-8 was actually 41 pounds lighter than the six. This was in keeping with the concept of the '55 Chevy which was, as Ed Cole said, "built around lighter components."

In 1974, *Special-Interest Autos* magazine asked Cole if there was any major breakthrough in the 265's design. Possibly, Cole said, it was "when we decided to make the precision cylinder blocks—the heart of the engine—by using an entirely different casting technique. We used the green-sand core for the valley between the bore. That is, for the 45-degree angle center, 90 degree total, we used a green-sand core to eliminate the dry-sand core, so that we could turn the block upside down. We cast it upside down, so the plate that holds the bore cores could be accurately located. This way, we could cast down to 5/32nds jacketed walls."

In the same *SIA* article, Harry Barr pointed out certain advantages of the Chevy 265 over the '55 Pontiac V-8: ". . . their design was heavier than ours. But they developed a sheetmetal rocker arm that we thought had possibilities. It hadn't been decided yet, but we jumped into that, and gave it to our manufacturing group. They determined that they could make stamped rocker arms with no machining whatever—just a metal stamping.

"We also lubricated it differently from Pontiac . . . with the oil coming up through the tappet, up through the hollow pushrod into the rocker arms, then over to lubricate both the ball and the pallet of the rocker arm. . . . These were all new ideas, and very good as far as automation was concerned. You never had to screw anything—just press these studs in."

Actually, the 265 was Chevy's second V-8, the first being the disastrous 1917 design. But this one was near-perfect. Overhead valves, high compression, light weight, and oversquare dimensions (3.75 × 3.00) made it efficient and powerful. Some 43 percent of 1955 Chevys were equipped with it—amazing for a make which hadn't offered a V-8 within recent memory. Horsepower was 162, or 180 with "Power Pack" (four-barrel Rochester carburetor and dual

The Turbo-Fire V-8 was bored out to 283 cid for 1957, would be a Chevy performance mainstay into the '70s.

exhausts, available on all models except wagons). In basic form, the 265 was both more potent and more economical than the rival Ford 262 or the Plymouth 260, and it outsold them easily. It had plenty of development room, too. For 1956, Chevrolet offered 205- and 225-bhp versions using four-barrel and dual four-barrel carbs, respectively.

The 283-cid V-8 of 1957

The great small-block Chevy V-8 reached its second important development plateau in 1957. While the 265 was retained as the "base" engine this model year, the big news was the new 283-cid enlargement, achieved by punching out bore to 3.88 inches. In its mildest tune it produced 185 bhp at 4600 rpm; a four-barrel carb brought this up to 220 bhp; two fours resulted in either 245 or 270; and Chevy's new "Ramjet" fuel injection system boosted output to no less than 250 or 283. The last was the ultimate, achieving the magic goal of one horsepower per cubic inch, and was offered with close-ratio three-speed manual transmission only.

The 283 "fuelie" was carefully developed for good reliability. Mechanical valve lifters substituted for hydraulics when FI was specified. Longer-reach spark plugs with metal deflection shields were used to protect wiring and plug caps from manifold heat. The top of the block was a thicker casting to prevent

cylinder wall distortion through over-tight hold-down bolts. Fuel passages were tapered, increasing in cross-sectional area toward the inlet ports and in the "ram's horn" exhaust manifold to provide better scavenging and increased volumetric efficiency. There was a new distributor, with breaker points directly above the shaft bearing to help reduce fluctuations in the gap setting. And the front and intermediate main bearings were 0.063-inch thicker.

Though made by GM's Rochester carburetor division, the Ramjet fuel injection system was designed almost entirely by the Engineering Staff, simplified for production by Harry Barr and Zora Arkus-Duntov. It consisted of three main components: fuel meter, manifold assembly, and air meter, replacing intake manifold and carburetor. The unit took in air first, then injected fuel directly into each intake port for mixing. The amount of fuel used was very precisely controlled, again for better volumetric efficiency and mileage. Cold-weather starting and warm-up were improved, and the unit by itself boosted output by about 5 bhp compared to the twin four-barrel carbureted engine. Chevrolet claimed that FI eliminated manifold icing, and reduced the tendency to stall when cornering hard.

A special two-piece aluminum manifold casting was used on 283 V-8s equipped with fuel injection. The upper casting contained air passages and air/fuel metering system bases, while the lower casting made

This SR-2 was one of several hot street/track Corvette prototypes built in 1957.

The last Corvette to offer the "fuelie" 283 was the '61, which featured new "ducktail" rear styling.

The type W "Turbo-Thrust" was Chevy's first big-block V-8, appeared on the 1958s like this Impala hardtop.

up ram tubes and covered the top center of the engine.

A major engineering development is never simple—or easy. And although the introduction of Ramjet injection was a milestone in Chevy's history, bugs were inevitable. At the Daytona Speed Weeks, for example, the fuel cut off during acceleration characteristic was eliminated because this created a flat spot in response. Fuel nozzles, too, required attention. They were extended further into the air stream to prevent them from absorbing too much heat and causing rough idling.

There were no formal published tests of the fuel-injected 283 in a standard Chevrolet, but performance of the "fuelie" in Corvettes is worth mentioning. The 0–60 mph acceleration times of the most potent versions consistently averaged just over 6 seconds, and top speeds were in the region of 140 mph. Driving a 250-bhp FI Corvette (33 bhp below the 1957 maximum), Walt Woron of *Motor Trend* magazine whizzed through the 0–60 sprint in just 7.2 seconds. With a special 283 sporting 10.5:1 compression, dual exhausts, special cam, and solid lifters, the car did 134 mph, and convinced Woron that even at that it wasn't really extended. Extrapolating from these results, a two-door sedan weighing about 400 pounds more than the 'Vette might have done 0–60 in about 8 seconds and hit a top of 120 mph with the right gearing.

The 348-cid V-8 of 1958

The first big-block Chevy V-8 was introduced in 1958 as an optional alternative to the small-block engine. It was not related in any way to its classic predecessor, being new from the ground up. Neither has it been regarded as one of the highlights in Chevy engine history. Although good in its way, it was simply out-classed by the "fuelie" 283 before it and by the 409 which took over at the head of the line for 1962. But the 348 was the largest and most powerful Chevrolet engine you could buy in 1958–61, and deserves at least a brief mention.

As the 265/283 was known as "Turbo-Fire," the 348 was dubbed "Turbo-Thrust," but the factory knew it

better as the "type W." This designation stemmed from the characteristic shape on the outside edge of the rocker covers, something that was much less unique as we moved into the '60s. The "W" was intended for the new generation of much larger and heavier Chevrolets born in 1958 that blossomed into the full-blown 119-inch-wheelbase cruisers of 1959.

With a bore and stroke of 4.125 × 3.25 inches and 9.5:1 compression ratio, the 348 developed 250 bhp at 4000 rpm and 355 pounds-feet of torque at 2800 rpm. Combustion chambers were cylindrical wedges formed by flat-bottom heads that rested against the block faces at a 16-degree angle. The cast-aluminum pistons were machined with 16-degree dual-sloping upper surfaces. Hydraulic valve lifters were used, as they were in the small-block V-8s (except fuel-injected units). "Because of the lack of restrictions to passage of the fuel [/air] mixture in the heads, and because half of the piston is closer to the head than the other half, turbulence is tremendous and volumetric efficiency should be excellent," observed *Motor Trend.* The "W" came standard with dual exhausts and four-barrel carburetor, but was not offered with fuel injection—something Chevy had had problems with, and was generally encouraging only for Corvettes.

The 348's highest stage of development appeared for 1960—two four-barrel carburetors good for a rated 355 horsepower. It continued in this form for the 1961 model year before disappearing in favor of the 409.

The 348 should be remembered not as a mighty powerhouse, but as a smooth and reliable big-block for the new, larger Impala. Its 10-second 0–60 mph capability was about the norm for 1958—hardly the kick-in-the-back acceleration provided by the FI or dual-quad 283s. Significantly, Chevrolet offered very little hop-up equipment for the "W" for the simple reason that it was never really intended as a high-performance mill. In 1958, of course, Chevrolet was outwardly abiding by the Automobile Manufacturers Association (AMA) decision to "discourage" (or at least not advertise) racing, and the 348 fit right in with the Division's public posture. Performance enthusiasts would have to be content with the hotter versions of the 283 through 1961. Happily, these powered some of the most memorable of the "performance" Chevys.

1955-57 Chevrolet:

The Once and Future Classic

Nearly two million 1955 Chevrolets were sold—which was no surprise. Completely new from the ground up, with pretty styling and the option of a potent V-8 engine, the '55 was the most important postwar Chevrolet to date. And notwithstanding the narrow meaning of the word when applied to prewar cars, it has become perhaps the most "classic" of all Chevys.

Tom McCahill of *Mechanix Illustrated* magazine called the new car "a junior-sized Olds with Buick doors and a Cadillac rear, the most glamorous-looking and hottest-performing Chevy to come down the pike." Floyd Clymer of *Popular Mechanics* added: "Best-handling Chevrolet I have ever driven, and it feels like a large car." The new Chevy was chosen to pace the Indy 500, and was picked by *Motor Trend* magazine (along with the '55 Mercury) as the best-handling car of the year. GM had succeeded in its goal of making the '55 excitingly different. Chevy's image as an "old man's car" was gone for good.

We have already discussed development of the 265 V-8 engine (Chapter II), certainly the most significant technical feature of the '55 model. Very much secondary, but still quite important, were the new car's tubular frame rails and Hotchkiss rear axle, both departures for Chevrolet. These aside, the mechanical spec was conventional. The independent front suspension consisted of coil springs and coaxial, life-sealed, double-acting shocks. The rear suspension used semi-elliptic leaf springs and diagonally mounted shock absorbers. The 15-inch wheels wore 6.70 four-ply tubeless tires, and the wheelbase was an almost-ideal 115 inches. Brakes were 11-inch hydraulic drums. Steering was by recirculating ball-nut with a 20:1 ratio. Optional as an alternative to Powerglide automatic was Borg-Warner overdrive, the first appearance of this unit on a GM car.

The 1955 Chevy was a styling sensation as well as an engineering *tour de force,* benefiting from the team put together by Harley Earl—Clare MacKichan, head of the Chevy styling studio, and Carl Renner, the talented designer responsible for the unique Nomad wagon.

It was Earl who chose the unorthodox, European-style eggcrate grille of the '55, and pushed it despite the prevailing desires of management, which wanted a more contemporary (in other words, chrome-laden) front end. They got it in 1956, but the '55 was strictly Earl's work. Some dealers didn't like it, saying they had a tough time selling a chrome-minded public on it compared to the flashy grillework of the rival Ford and Plymouth. But with hindsight, we know that Harley Earl had a truly elegant idea. The grille was neat, efficient, beautifully simple—which flew in the face of the industry's preference for gaudiness. It was one of the leading reasons the 1955 Chevy was such a styling standout.

The notched beltline, also new for 1955, was first

Chevrolet general manager Thomas Keating (seated) and Indy chairman Tony Hulman, Jr. with the 1955 pace car.

Wide, chromy grille was originally planned for '55, appeared on the facelifted '56 Chevy.

seen on 1953 specials, like the Buick Skylark and Cadillac Eldorado, and was common on the larger GM products of 1954. This, too, was a Harley Earl innovation. "He liked low roofs," remembered Clare MacKichan. "That is why you see thick sheetmetal. He liked low windows—none of these cars have very huge windows, like you see on the road today. He liked very low rear quarters, so to get that feeling he wanted to raise the rear fender, and sometimes it was higher than

the beltline at this point. That is how we got into that kind of dipped shape."

Carl Renner points out that Earl's physical stature had much to do with his ideas: "He was six-foot four, and mock-ups looked quite different to him than they would to an average-sized person. On-the-job designers, in order to view their efforts as Earl did, strapped blocks of wood to their shoes . . . all unknown to Mr. Earl, of course."

The 1955 Bel Air hardtop as it might have looked to styling chief Harley Earl. Note "saddleback" two-toning.

Bel Air convertible was the top of the 1955 Chevy line. Dipped beltline was borrowed from larger GM cars.

Two-toning—not only on the roof but also on part of the body—was an essential for the 1955 Chevrolet, because it sold cars in the middle '50s. It was fairly daring on Bel Air models, with the roof color extending over the rear deck and upper rear fenders, separated from the second body color by a stainless-steel molding. Lesser models had a less elaborate arrangement.

Hooded headlamps were also a popular styling idea at the time, and these were nicely blended in to the '55 package. Likewise, the design team created attractive, functional taillights that could be seen from the sides as well as the rear. The lights jutted out from the fenders, and were originally intended to define a prominent horizontal crease in the rear deck. This did not emerge in production, probably due to the extra expense it would have entailed. Even so, the rear-end design was of a high order, and still looks pleasing today.

The 1955 Chevrolet line comprised 150, 210, and Bel Air series offering a choice of 16 different models and nine different power teams, plus an array of bright, bold colors. Interiors were finished in complementing hues carefully keyed to the exteriors. The driver faced a completely redesigned "twin-cowl" instrument panel inspired by the Corvette. Decorating the Bel Air dash were 987 "bow-tie" Chevy logos—a design idea developed by Renner as a constant reminder of what you were driving. The hood mascot, a winged bird, was another Chevy trademark—Renner designed all the hood ornaments from 1953 through '56.

Without doubt the most interesting '55 Chevy was the beautiful Nomad, part of the Bel Air series. Like all things at GM, this was the result of another Harley Earl idea—combining the best attributes of hardtop and station wagon. The first Nomad was a showcar, with lower body lines taken from the first Corvette, mounted on a conventional '53 wagon chassis. This was displayed to considerable acclaim at the 1954 GM Motorama, and was the basis of the production design. The Motorama Nomad had a fiberglass body, while the production '55s were all-steel, of course.

The Nomad roofline was Carl Renner's work. Commencing with a distinctive, wide, slanted B-pillar, it terminated in a thin C-pillar raked at precisely the same angle. Curved rear glass helped eliminate blind spots. On the showcar the rear glass dropped into the tailgate,

1955 Two-Ten Sport Coupe. Note optional grille guard.

Corvette-based Nomad showcar, first seen at '54 Motorama.

Positive reception to Corvette Nomad led to the production '55 based on that year's new passenger car styling.

but production Nomads used a more conventional two-piece gate.

The Nomad's decorative chrome tailgate trim, often referred to as "bananas," was part of GM Styling's quest for interesting "graphics" that would make the car stand out. The grooves in the rear roof were strictly decorative, though at one time Harley Earl had considered a telescoping retractable roof panel, which would have had a similar appearance when closed. It was dropped due to cost and doubts about its practicality, particularly water sealing. Even so, Nomad "R&D" wasn't quite perfect—the cars suffered chronic leaks around the tailgate.

Virtually every road tester liked the styling of the 1955 Chevy. It seemed more "deluxe" than rival Plymouth, more distinctive than that year's Ford. Performance, of course, was expected because of the new V-8 engine. But the biggest surprise was the car's fine handling. "That mushy feeling, so long associated with the American automobile, is gone," wrote Walt Woron in *Motor Trend*. "In its place is beginning to emerge a feeling of solid sureness, a willingness to be steered, not aimed . . . We didn't have to correct the

wheel on a straight road unless there was a crown . . . easy to steer, even with our fingers (and this wasn't a power-steering car) . . . when we deliberately drove it off the shoulder the car would move aside, but wouldn't whip so as to cause us to lose control . . . the same thing happened on street-car tracks and ruts. . . . There wasn't any wheel vibration until we started over rough roads. We could throw it into corners at practically any speed . . . even through turns that would make most other cars quail. . . . "

The V-8-equipped '55s were everything the testers expected they would be. A standard 162-bhp Bel Air with Powerglide driven by Floyd Clymer topped 108 mph. And the 180-bhp version was even better. *Motor Trend* wound one such car from rest to 60 mph in 11.4 seconds (using Low range only), did the standing quarter mile in 18.4, and clocked the 50–80 mph spurt (holding Low to 60 mph) in 12.9 seconds. This sort of performance was most comparable to a 1954 Cadillac—and no Chevrolet had run with a Cadillac in history. This was big news in 1955.

All this performance inevitably led to competition, beginning with that year's Daytona Speed Weeks in February. Matched against the likes of Chrysler 300s, Buicks, and Oldsmobiles, Jack Radtke's Chevy finished tenth overall. Chevys captured the four top spots in their class, occupying eight of the first 11 positions. In the two-way measured mile for cars of 250–299 cubic inches, Chevys took three of the first five positions. Soon "Smokey" Yunick entered a V-8 in NASCAR short-track races. Driven by famed former Hudson pilot Herb Thomas, it was unconquerable. Even in the longer Grand National events it was formidable, with Thomas and Fonty Flock often winning against much larger and more powerful machinery. In short-track competition, nobody could catch it.

Ed Cole, observing these early NASCAR exploits, made certain "export" (actually competition) parts

Fullsize clay model for the production 1955 Nomad.

available for Chevrolet. That's when Yunick began preparing his cars in earnest. Chevrolet performance peaked at Darlington, South Carolina, on Labor Day 1955 at the Southern 500. Of the 69 starters, 24 were Chevrolets, and they dominated the event. Thomas crossed the line first, averaging 92.281 mph, followed by Jim Reed in another Chevy. Tim Flock was third in a Chrysler 300—but Chevys were also fourth, seventh, eighth, ninth, and tenth. That's seven of the first ten places—not a bad day's work! These were 195-bhp cars, essentially stock Power-Pack V-8s with the addition of Corvette camshafts and valve springs. Rear axle ratios were usually selected for the particular race, but they were all "off the shelf." Chevy kept winning—at Charlotte, North Carolina, in October, and in AAA events with the skilled Marshall Teague driving. In all, 1955 was the greatest competition showing for a low-priced car within anyone's memory.

On the strength of this impressive showing it wasn't hard for the Division to come up with a new slogan for '56: "The Hot One's Even Hotter." This wasn't meaningless hype, either. In September 1955, driving a Bel Air sport sedan with a 205-bhp Super Turbo-Fire V-8, Chevy's Zora Arkus-Duntov charged up Pikes Peak in 17 minutes, 24.05 seconds to establish a new American stock-sedan record—fully two minutes faster than the previous best time. Tom McCahill judged the '56 Chevy the "best performance buy in the world . . . it would whiz by a Duesenberg like Halley's Comet, and the vacuum as it went by would suck the stork off a Hispano-Suiza." Another magazine called it "as quick and sure-footed as a cat," thanks to its 14 percent increase in horsepower and improved handling.

What prospective buyers saw first, of course, was styling, so GM tried to make the '56 as visually different from the '55 as possible. It was an expensive facelift: some $40 million went into body redesign—a million dollars alone on new, crisper fenders. In general, the body was "bulked up," but it didn't look heavy. The '55 model's basic simplicity of line was maintained.

The controversial Ferrari-style grille was dropped for a more contemporary latticework spanning the full width of the car and incorporating large parking lights. "We had two cars out at the proving grounds with

Facelifted 1956 Chevys were bulkier without looking heavy or gaudy. Shown is the Bel Air Sport Coupe.

1956 Two-Ten Sport Coupe.

1956 Bel Air convertible, as desireable today as it was new.

different grilles for the '55 program," said Clare MacKichan—"the Earl design and a wider one . . . this wider '56 grille design was the result of people not accepting the narrow grille." The new grille was integrated with a flatter, longer hood, which emphasized the low, wide, rectangular look of the '56. A new hood ornament and headlight eyebrows were substituted. Along the sides, revised trim moldings and two-toning dictated reshaped wheel openings, now flared and elongated. Said Renner, "I like the '56 side treatment. It is not as heavy as the '57. It has a lot of visual zip."

But the '56 was definitely busier than the '55, especially at the rear. The simple '55 taillights, for example, were replaced by complicated units incorporating round taillights and backup lights in a white-metal sculpture. The one on the left was hinged at the top, and cleverly hid the fuel filler. Overall, GM designers held the 1955 treatment the better-looking. Some customers apparently did too: before long customizers were replacing the '56 taillights with plain red lenses, which must have made filling the gas tank a complicated procedure. Even so, Chevrolet was being quite conservative—stylists shunned, for example, the wildly uplifted fenders of that year's Dodge and Plymouth.

The 1956 line was again composed of 150, 210, and Bel Air trim levels, spanning 19 different models available with a choice of 11 power teams and 10 solid colors or 14 two-tones. New this year was a four-door hardtop for 210 and Bel Air advertised as "embodying the youthful lines of a convertible, the practicality of a hardtop, and the convenience of a four-door sedan." Growing public interest also caused Chevrolet to expand station wagon offerings to six by adding a four-door, nine-passenger 210 Beauville and enlarging the Bel Air Beauville from six- to nine-passenger capacity. The rest of the '56 lineup remained as for 1955.

Although width and height remained the same, the '56 Chevys were longer than the '55s by 2–3 inches. The extra length and new side treatment gave them a much more streamlined look. Inside, the basic dash configuration was unaltered, but the Bel Air's "bow-tie" motif was abandoned in favor of rectangular slots. "You get a whole generation of 'bow ties' and you've had enough," MacKichan said.

One of the salient developments of the year was the transposition of the Ford and Chevy images. These arch rivals had gambled for years on performance (Ford) and reliability (Chevrolet). But for 1956, Ford went on its celebrated safety binge, while Chevrolet emphasized performance. It paid off—for Chevy, which outsold Ford by nearly 200,000 units for the model year.

Both Chevrolet's six and V-8s were more powerful for '56. The 235.5-cid "Blue Flame 140" replaced both the 123- and 136-bhp sixes of 1955, and could be ordered with standard, overdrive, or Powerglide

Four-door hardtop bodystyle was a new addition for '56.

Pillarless four-door was dubbed Sport Sedan.

1956 Bel Air Sport Sedan. A 210 version was also offered.

Bel Air Beauville wagon got a third seat for '56.

transmissions. Compression ratio was now 8:1, up from 7.5:1 in 1955, and the six produced 210 pounds-feet of torque at 4200 rpm. The 265 V-8 still gave 162 bhp with manual transmission, but a higher-lift cam raised output on Powerglide models to 170 bhp and torque to 257 lbs-ft at 3300 rpm. The "Power-Pack" option (higher-lift cam, 9.25:1 compression, four-barrel carb, special intake manifolds, and dual exhausts) yielded 205 bhp. The ultimate '56 Turbo-Fire was the same engine with dual four-barrels, and developed 225 bhp.

Suspension changes were also made. Coil spring length was increased and spring rates decreased to reduce the tendency to nosedive. Rear springs had wider hangers, which allowed more rubber in the bushing to resist compression from axle side thrusts. Six-leaf rear springs were standard on the nine-passenger Beauville, and available for other wagons at extra cost. Optional equipment for all models included power steering, power brakes, power windows, power seat, and air conditioning. A variety of minor accessories were added—rear-mounted radio antenna and exterior spare tire were two of the most popular.

The swanky Nomad was restyled along with the rest of the '56 line. It had sold just 8350 copies in 1955, partly because it had been introduced late. Chevy now hoped sales would pass the 10,000 mark. A few of the '56 Nomad's features were unique to this year. The angle of the vertical quarter molding trim was reversed to match the angle of the slanted B-pillar. Small chrome "Vs" exclusive to the Nomad were placed beneath its taillights (other Chevys signified a V-8 with a single "V" on the trunk or tailgate). Seat inserts were now the same as those on Bel Air hardtops and the

1956 Bel Air Nomad, one of only 8103 built.

Beauville wagon—the quilted inserts from the previous year were abandoned.

As in 1955, *Motor Trend* named Nomad one of the year's most beautiful cars, though admitted the styling did have its shortcomings: "Its distinct personal-car feel forces certain limiting features . . . the low roofline, compact overall package, sharply sloping rear." Sadly, production dropped rather than rose: only 8103 of the '56 models were built. The main reasons were that the Nomad was expensive in relation to other wagons, and suffered (from a marketing standpoint) by having just two doors, not four.

With so many stages of tune offered for '56, there were vast performance differences among V-8 Chevys. The basic 170-bhp version with Powerglide recorded 0–60 mph in 11.9 seconds and a 98-mph top speed in *Motor Life* magazine's road test. A 205-bhp test car ran 0–60 in 8.9 seconds, and had a 109-mph top

Nomad shared in the 1956 facelift, acquired several trim features unique to this one model.

Costly facelift on the '55 bodyshell and new 283 V-8 highlighted the 1957 Chevrolets, like this Bel Air convertible.

speed. A wide array of axle ratios allowed the customer to pick the level of performance desired. To get a 17.5-second quarter mile in 1955, for example, you needed the 190-bhp engine and a 4.11 rear axle. The 1956 car with the 205-bhp engine and a more tractable 3.70 axle would be a second faster.

Competition results proved the merit of the '56 Chevy. Returning to Darlington, a 210 lapped the track at an average of 101.58 mph in a 24-hour endurance run, beating the previous U.S. production car record held by Chrysler by 11.69 mph. In July, three cars prepared by Chevy Engineering under Vince Piggins (a recent arrival from Hudson) were entered in the annual Pikes Peak Hillclimb, where Chevys finished first, second, fifth, sixth, and tenth. Jerry Unser Jr., driving the number-one car, leaped to the summit in 16:08 minutes, 1:16 better than Duntov's impressive 1955 showing. Truly, the "Hot One" *was* even hotter for '56.

But it was only a warmup for what was to come.

For 1957, Chevy's V-8s offered horsepower ranging from 162 to 283, using 265- and 283-cid displacements. The latter was achieved by boring the block out to 3.875 inches. Fuel injection (see Chapter II) and multiple carburetion were available, along with higher compression and a higher-lift cam. Mechanical lifters were used on "fuelie" engines. All V-8s had longer-reach spark plugs, tapered fuel passages, and thicker castings for the top of the block (to discourage cylinder wall distortion). Other changes common to both 265s and 283s were new carburetor fuel filters, larger ports, wider bearings, stainless-steel expanders in oil-control piston rings, heat deflection shields to protect spark plug leads, and a relocated choke to improve hot starting. Where ordered, dual exhausts came with a new balance tube that equalized flow through the mufflers and made the life of both exhaust

Two-Ten Beauville nine-passenger model was one of six wagons in Chevy's 1957 lineup.

1957 Bel Air was marked by brushed aluminum side trim and gracefully finned rear fenders.

Massive bumper/grille made the facelifted '57 Chevy look new. Many think it's the best looking of the '55-'57 models.

systems approximately the same.

Several mechanical changes were instituted for V-8 models. Clutches with higher torque ratings were specified for the 265 and the six, while 283s with four-barrel carbs or fuel injection got a semi-centrifugal clutch. There was a new distributor for all V-8s and a relocated voltage regulator. Battery and line fuses were used in lamp circuits if an accessory junction block was not installed.

May 1954 clay shows origins of '57 front end.

Besides fuel injection, Chevy's other major engineering innovation for 1957 was its new Turboglide automatic transmission, offered optionally with 283 V-8s. Lighter than Powerglide by 82 pounds, it had three turbines and two planetary gearsets in combination with a variable-pitch stator and conventional torque converter pump. It embodied a passing gear through the stator. Flooring the accelerator increased the turbine blade angle to deliver greater torque to the output shaft.

Rear axle gearing, chassis, and brakes were revised for '57. Ratios were now 3.34:1 for automatic, 3.55 for manual, and 4.11 (retained from '56) for overdrive. Wheelbase stayed at 115 inches, but overall length was now almost 17 feet, so the frame was accordingly beefed up with new front braces. New power control-arm ball joint and seal assemblies were adopted for the front suspension, shocks were revised to match the new chassis weight, and the rear leaf springs were moved farther outboard to improve roadholding. Finally, Chevy switched to 14-inch tires following an industry trend that year, mainly in the interest of a lower, longer look.

As the third and final edition of the "classic" Chevy, the '57 received an extensive and again costly facelift designed to keep up with the times, pending the complete redesign scheduled for 1958. "We were as

1957 Two-Tens like this Sport Sedan shared Bel Air side trim motif, but had a painted insert.

Late-1954 proposal for 1957 facelift.

1957 Bel Air four-door sedan

extreme as we could be," MacKichan said, "while saving the deck, roof, and doors. . . . We did such obvious things as moving taillights to a new location, changing that whole corner. From the side we did a similar thing with the aluminum panel and trim molding."

Up front, the car's appearance was entirely new. A massive bumper surrounding a concave grille had been evident in styling sketches as early as 1949, and this now emerged in production. The bumper/grille was tremendously expensive according to MacKichan and Renner, but that was allowable because of a large budget—in 1955, it would have been prohibitive.

Every detail of the '57 Chevy was crafted for a lower, longer appearance. The car was 2.5 inches longer and 1.5 inches lower, the latter a benefit of the smaller wheels and wider, lower-pressure tires. A new ventilation system, with air intakes nestling above the headlamps, helped reduce cowl height (air was routed to the interior through long, concealed ducts). The hood was dressed up with twin windsplits instead of the hood ornament of previous years, and emphasized the bulky new bumper/grille.

Along the sides the design objective was to retain the 1955–56 door and roof boundaries while creating a new look. Styling Staff's solution here was brilliant. Side decoration on all models was handled by discreet

flashes of brightwork—intersecting vertical and horizontal bars on the rear of 150s, a straight bar splitting into a forward-pointing triangle on 210s, the same thing on Bel Airs with the triangle filled by brushed aluminum. A longtime favorite of Harley Earl, brushed aluminum was expensive, but it did wonders for the Bel Air's looks.

The Nomad took easily to the facelift, but the model was in what would be its final year as a distinctive hardtop-wagon. Only 6534 were sold, the lowest for its three-year production run. Trim was standardized with

1957 Bel Air convertible and Two-Ten Sport Sedan

1957 saw the last of the "true" Nomad wagons.

Redesigned gauge cluster featured on all 1957 Chevys.

Bel Airs except for Nomad script and a small gold "V" on V-8 tailgates. But the handsome roof styling blended gracefully with the revised lower body contours, complementing the massive bumper/grille and the finny new rear fenders.

All 1957 Chevrolets featured a redesigned dashboard, with the instruments clustered under the steering wheel and the radio speaker moved to a central position on top. Seats and door panels wore new trim. 210s used patterned cloth and vinyl (all vinyl on the Delray hardtop). Bel Airs were dressed in Jacquard loomed cloth combined with vinyl, and their floors were carpeted.

Chevrolet's forte in 1957 was, of course, straightline performance. A typical 0–60 mph time for the base 185-bhp 283 (a single 162-bhp 265 was offered as the base V-8) was 11 seconds. The 270-bhp version would do it in 8.2 seconds, while the hairy engines (245/270-bhp dual four-barrel, 250/283-bhp "fuelie") would bring this into the 6–7 second range. Turboglide cars were praised as being "almost turbine smooth," with completely unobtrusive shifting and good engine braking.

Though GM's fuel injection suffered from reliability problems and slow acceptance by the public, it performed well for Chevrolet during the 1957 racing season. In late 1956, an "independent engineering firm," Southern Engineering Development Company (SEDCO), was formed under Vince Piggins' direction with tacit assistance from Chevrolet. Piggins and team manager Dick Rathmann arrived at Daytona 1957 with a stable of cars. In Class 4 (213–259 cid), Chevy took the first three places in the two-way flying mile. Then, in competition for four-barrel carb/automatic transmission models, Chevrolet scored a 1-2-3 sweep. In the measured-mile acceleration runs, Chevys dominated their class, taking the *first 18 places*—and even the six-cylinder models showed well in their class. The make swept the Pure Oil manufacturer's championship with a point count of 574, far ahead of runner-up Ford's 309 and Mercury at 174.

Unfortunately, this promising start was to be cut short. While Chevrolet was running at Daytona, the Automobile Manufacturer's Association was meeting at Detroit in response to an appeal from the National Safety Council, the AAA (now out of racing), and

Jack Smith in the number 47 Chevy on the oval dirt track at Daytona, pursued by Banjo Matthews and Darel Dieringer.

Bob Wellborn's '57 Chevy outruns Curtis Turner's Ford in an early NASCAR convertible race at Daytona.

Paul Goldsmith puts his Chevy back on course at Daytona's beach oval track in 1957.

several of its own members. These parties were insisting that the "horsepower race" and the emphasis on competition in auto advertising were breeding a generation of dangerous, accident-prone drivers. A resolution was prepared recommending that manufacturers henceforth not participate in competition, nor supply pace cars, nor use race results in advertising. In June, the AMA passed this resolution unanimously.

To some extent, there was good reason for this "recommendation" (it was not an outright ban, as is often thought). There was, primarily, the threat of Congressional action—notably a tax on high-power cars. And, as author Paul Van Valkenburgh has pointed out, the AMA itself was made up of representatives from companies like Kaiser, Studebaker-Packard, AMC, Mack Truck, White, and International Harvester to whom racing meant nothing whatsoever.

Piggins recalls that he kept the racing parts business alive because of continued demand for "export" or heavy-duty components by private individuals. Indeed, Chevrolet did not fade away either on the drag strips or on the tracks. At the 1957 Southern 500 at Darlington, South Carolina, on Labor Day, Speedy Thompson brought his '57 Chevy home at a 100-mph average. Even in 1958 the beat went on: that year's Southern was captured by a year-old Chevy driven by Fireball Roberts, who averaged 102.6 mph. (It happened again the following year, too, as Jim Reed won in a 1959

Chevrolet.) Piggins even published a booklet, after the AMA decision, entitled "1957 Chevrolet Stock Car Competition Guide." This detailed just about everything anybody needed to make a stormer out of his Chevy— HD equipment; special modifications for engine, chassis and body; how to set up a car for track work; competition tuning; spare parts; even data on how to register a race car, complete with addresses. The result was a continued stream of very highly competitive, often formidable Chevrolet stock cars. This continued until the AMA "ban" began to be ignored with increasing regularity, first by Ford, later by General Motors. By the time the next generation of super-stock Chevys was taking form in 1961, the marque had won the allegiance of hundreds of competitors, both amateur and professional. The old, pre-1955 conservative image was gone forever.

A lot of people would remember the "classic" 1955–57 Chevys. Indeed, almost five million of the cars were produced, and just about everybody has had one once. There is more to their popularity today than sheer performance, however. Perhaps the biggest appeal is their clean, lithe styling, usually considered among the best American designs of those years, and never uninteresting. But it was PERFORMANCE, written in big, bold capital letters, that indelibly etched the 1955–57 Chevrolets in the public's mind. And in virtually every year after that, Chevy would have something for those who liked fast, able automobiles.

One of the first Chevys to wear the Super Sport tag was this showcar, a mildly modified production '57 Corvette. Note non-standard bodyside scoops and "double-bubble" racing windscreens.

Corvette came of age in 1956, and kept getting better with each passing year. The 1956–57 series set a new standard among sports cars for styling, performance, and convenience. The 1958–60 models with even more potent V-8s gave performance right up with the best of Europe's grand touring cars. The 1961–62 versions introduced the first elements of Bill Mitchell's thinking with their neat, sculpted tails.

The 1956 Corvette's design roots were in three showcars, the Biscayne hardtop and the LaSalle II sedan and roadster. These specials inspired the toothy new '56 grille and the unique concave sculpture on the sides. The Mercedes-Benz 300SL "gullwing" coupe was also an influence, lending its twin bulges to the Corvette's hood and the shape of its front fenderlines. All these elements came together in a beautiful package, one that was so good it would continue in

basically the same form through 1960, and with the new Mitchell tail through 1962.

Besides nice styling, the all-new '56 Corvette offered several improvements designed to challenge the Thunderbird's passenger comfort among the "boulevardier" types who bought two-seaters more for looks than performance. Visibility was improved, the windows rolled up instead of being attached by hand, and an optional hardtop gave sedan-like weather protection.

The 1956 engine was the basic Chevy 265 V-8, with four-barrel carburetor, 9.25:1 compression ratio, and a high-lift cam developed by Zora Arkus-Duntov. It put out 225 bhp and 270 foot-pounds of torque. With manual gearbox and standard 3.55:1 rear axle ratio, the car would turn 0–60 mph in 7.5 seconds and 16-second quarter miles. The steering was quick,

Biscayne showcar (left) inspired the concave "cove" used on the redesigned 1956 Corvette.

1956-62 Corvette:

America's Sports Car Grows Up

weight distribution nearly perfect.

The 1957 Corvette looked much like the '56, but had many under-the-skin changes. A new 283 V-8 and four-speed gearbox option arrived. The 283 could be had in various guises (see previous chapters) with up to "one HP per cubic inch" in fuel-injected form. The FI had its bugs, but when running properly it gave Corvette 0–60 mph performance in the 6-second range and staggering dragstrip acceleration. Even better performance could be had by adding the four-speed gearbox and stump-puller 4.11 rear axle, which lowered the 0–60 time by a second, yet still provided a 130-mph top speed.

So equipped, the '57 Corvette was a genuine race-and-ride sports car. A pair of production models finished 12th and 15th at Sebring that year, first and second in their GT class, and 20 laps ahead of the nearest 300SL. These cars benefited from a newly announced Chevrolet RPO (Regular Production Option) designed just for competition: a package including front anti-sway bar and heavier springs all around, larger and firmer shocks, ceramic-metallic brake linings, finned brake drums, limited-slip differential, and quick-ratio steering.

Undoubtedly, the 1957 edition marked the Corvette's arrival as a true sports car that could earn respect from the *cognoscenti* as well as the kids. One European writer said, "Before Sebring, where we actually saw it for ourselves, the Corvette was regarded as a plastic toy. After Sebring, even the most biased were forced to admit that the Americans had one of the world's finest sports cars—as capable on the track

1956 Corvette sported a noticeably cleaner front end.

Lift-off hardtop was a new comfort feature for '56.

as it was on the road. Those who drove and understood the Corvette could not help but reach that conclusion."

GM had paused to consider whether to continue the

Corvette "father" Zora Arkus-Duntov in 1957 piloting the Sebring SS racer. Its competition career was short-lived.

Team manager John Fitch (left) and Duntov inspect the race-ready SS before Sebring 1957.

Corvette after 1955; there was no question about its future after 1957. Model year production had gone from 3467 for '56 to 6339 for '57. It rose again to 9168 the following year. But for the car to survive, it would have to make money, and through 1957 it had not. Sales volume was the order of the day.

After the AMA decision to deemphasize racing (see Chapter III), GM began taking a softer approach to the Corvette, promoting it more as a comfortable touring car than fire-breathing sportster. The 1958 model received the quad headlight treatment and more glitter typical of the era, but it was still quite fast, and would

Twin decklid chrome strips marked the 1958 'Vette . . .

. . . so did quad headlights and fake hood louvers.

continue to be so. When you have a machine that will reach 60 mph from standstill in seven seconds, whatever additional performance you wring out of it is merely academic. Furthermore, Corvettes continued to compete, albeit without direct GM sponsorship. By the time 1962 rolled around, Chevrolet had the most powerful sports car in its history.

Functional improvements accompanied the added brightwork for '58. Instruments were regrouped in a cluster directly in front of the driver for better readability. A large grab bar was put ahead of the passenger, and seatbelts were made standard. The fuel injection system was reworked for greater reliability, and that year's "fuelie" engines delivered 250 or 290 bhp. Output on carburetor 283s ranged from 230 to 270 bhp. The heavy-duty suspension option was retained. Corvettes won the SCCA B-production championship in both 1958 and '59.

Styling for 1959–60 was mainly a continuation of the '58 look, except for removal of the fake louvers from the hood. Among detail changes, inside door knobs were moved forward to avoid snagging on clothes, the shift lever received a lock out T-handle, and the clutch was given a wider range of adjustment. Chevy's RPO handling option now had harder spring settings, and radius rods were fitted to the rear suspension on all models to reduce axle tramp.

The 1960 Corvette might have been a completely new car—the stillborn Q-model with a 94-inch wheelbase, all-independent suspension, and a rear-mounted transaxle. Though the Q-model's styling did accurately forecast the 1963 Sting Ray, difficult times in the industry precluded its production. The 1960 Corvette was therefore just a revision of the '59 car. However, it did feature wider use of aluminum—in clutch housings and some radiators and in cylinder heads of fuel-injected engines. The aluminum heads were fine in theory, but suffered failures from internal

1959 Corvette was cleaner. Power options were unchanged.

1959-60 'Vettes looked the same. This is a '59.

Bill Mitchell's XP-700 showcar toured the country in 1960.

flaws in practice. They also tended to warp if the engine overheated. Accordingly, they were soon deleted from the parts list. Zora Arkus-Duntov replaced the stiff-spring set-up that year with double sway bars that improved ride and handling significantly. There were also minor changes to the interior.

In 1960, Corvette reached a new performance pinnacle at the LeMans 24-hour race. Three cars entered by Briggs Cunningham in the big-engine GT class were excellent performers. One achieved 151 mph on the Mulsanne straight. The lead car, driven by Bob Grossman and John Fitch, finished a respectable eighth. If Sebring '57 hadn't sufficiently impressed the Europeans, LeMans '60 did.

The 1958–61 period saw the last of the small-block Corvette V-8s, and no less than seven variations were offered:

Years	bhp/rpm	induction	CR
1958–61	230/4800	1 4bbl	9.5
1958–61	245/5000	1 4bbl	9.5
1958–59	250/5000	fuel inj.	9.5
1958–61	270/6000	2 4bbl	9.5
1958–59	290/6200	fuel inj.	10.5
1960–61	275/5200	fuel inj.	11.0
1960–61	315/6200	fuel inj.	11.0

Corvette styling for 1961–62 was a mild facelift of 1958–60, but a highly effective one. By now, Bill Mitchell had replaced Harley Earl as chief of GM design. Mitchell had created the racing Stingray, which then inspired the XP-700 showcar, and both featured a distinctive ducktail rear end. On the showcar, this was attached to a front end and midsection like that of the 1958–60 model. The result was received favorably by the public, and was accordingly put into production. To help make the '61 look fresher still, Mitchell did

away with the grille teeth that had marked Corvettes since 1953, replacing them with a subdued mesh. Stylists also painted headlamp rims the same color as the body for a cleaner look.

Prices, meanwhile, had been climbing upward. The Corvette had listed for $3149 base in 1956; in 1958 it was $3631, and in 1960 $3872. For 1961 the total was $3934, and in 1962 it moved over the $4000 mark. Fuel-injected cars could, of course, run some $1500 above the basic list price of the original 1953 model. Nevertheless, Corvette buyers continued to get a lot of car for the money. In 1961, for example, Chevrolet adopted an aluminum radiator, along with such standard equipment items as a parking brake warning light, dual sunvisors, interior lights, and windshield washers.

Facelifted '61 Corvette borrowed XP-700 ducktail rear.

'Vette lost grille teeth for '61 in favor of "mesh mouth."

Engine options for 1961 were unchanged from the previous year, but the four-speed transmission housing was now made of aluminum also, and a wider choice of ratios was offered for the three-speed gearbox. By this time, over 85 percent of Corvette buyers were ordering manual shift, with a two-to-one preference for four-speeds.

The hairy 315-bhp injected engine was truly impressive when coupled to high-winding rear axle ratios. This powerplant and the 4.11:1 gearset gave a 0–60 mph leap of just 5.5 seconds and a 14-second quarter mile at 100 mph. And it would still see the car to 130 mph!

Model year 1962 was the last for the second-generation Corvette, and in many ways it was the best. Bill Mitchell now completed his styling refinements, emphasizing clean form instead of decoration. The trademark bodyside "cove" was toned down by omitting its chrome outline molding, the little bright teeth in the reverse side scoops were replaced with a modest grid, and the grille mesh was finished in black. One new piece of trim was added, a ribbed anodized-aluminum appliqué laid over each rocker panel. Stiff springs were reinstated as an RPO, and with their help, the great Dr. Dick Thompson won the SCCA A-production championship for Chevy.

Off the track, progress continued. Semon E. "Bunkie" Knudsen replaced upward-bound Ed Cole as Chevrolet general manager, and began to push for higher production across the board. For Corvette, this meant a sales drive that resulted in 14,531 cars for the model year compared to 10,939 in 1961.

Corvette had turned the profit corner.

The '62 edition was also one of the year's world-class performers. New that season was the soon-to-be immortal 327-cid V-8 (see Chapter VII), produced by enlarging the 283 block to a 4.00 × 3.25-inch bore and stroke. The fuel injection system was modified to suit the new dimensions, and a 3.08:1 rear axle ratio was added to the option list (lower-horsepower engines only) for quiet, smooth touring. This fine new V-8 formed the basis for Corvette power through 1965. It was offered in four forms for 1962–63— 250–340 bhp with carburetion, and 360 bhp with fuel injection. Its impressive torque gave the '62 models superior mid-range performance compared with their predecessors. They were also lightning-quick in the quarter-mile drag: typically, a 327 car with the 3.70 axle could turn it in 15 seconds at over 100 mph.

With the 1962 model, Chevy had reached a new peak in the Corvette's continuing, ever-exciting development. Thanks to men like Ed Cole and Zora Arkus-Duntov, "America's only true sports car" had matured into a fast, good-handling machine with clean, functional styling—easily the cleanest Corvette since 1956. But it would be totally eclipsed just one year later by the fabulous Sting Ray. Yet as revolutionary as it was, the Sting Ray owed a great deal to the successful evolution of the 1956–62 Corvettes. Maybe that's why the second-generation cars today command a wide and loyal following. An even better reason is that they're just as much a blast to drive now as they were when new—and there's no better recommendation than that for any performance car.

Last of the second-generation Corvettes was the 1962 model. Less chrome, blackout grille, and new 327 V-8 were featured.

The "flying dentist," Dr. Dick Thompson, on the way to the SCCA A-production championship in his 1962 'Vette.

1955 Corvette V-8—The first performance Chevy

Above: 1955 Bel Air   Below: 1956 Nomad   Inset: 1956 Bel Air

Above and Below: 1957 Bel Air   Insets: The '57 dash (left) and 283 V-8 (right)

Above and Inset: 1957 Bel Air   Below: The fuel-injected 283 V-8

Above: 1956 Corvette   Below: 1960 Impala

Above and Below: 1962 Bel Air (Hayden Proffitt replica drag car)

1963 Corvette Sting Ray (modified)

Above: 1963 Corvette Sting Ray   Below: 1964 Corvair Monza Spyder

1958-61 Impala:

From Super Highway to Super Sport

Chevy got an all-new bodyshell for 1958, but it would last only one year. Shown is the convertible version of the new Impala, officially a trim option for the top-line Bel Air series.

Aside from the Corvette, the big standard-size V-8 cars represented Chevy performance in the lean years immediately following the 1957 AMA decision against racing. So let's take a look at the hottest and most popular model of the period, the luxurious Impala.

"In 1959 we went to a shared bodyshell with Pontiac, Olds, and Buick," Clare MacKichan said. "The idea was to make the outer surfaces different so that nobody would know they were shared, but the things underneath that cost the major amount of money *would* be shared." Thus, the 1958 Chevy was a one-year design—not by choice, but by chance. Looking back, it was a pretty good one. Despite Detroit's almost universal fascination with the tailfin, Chevy designers shunned it for a new low-slung shape with lots of curves. They'd get to fins soon enough.

The Impala was first conceived as a "Bel Air Executive Coupe" for 1955. It fit in better though with the 1958 design concept, which dictated a longer, lower, and wider car. Officially, it was part of the Bel Air series, but more luxuriously finished inside and out. It

could be distinguished immediately from the standard Bel Air hardtop by its stainless steel rocker panels, special emblems, spinner hubcaps, and dummy "pitchfork" scoops ahead of the rear wheels. Two body styles were offered: two-door hardtop with six or 283 V-8 and convertible with V-8 only. The standard V-8 for '58 was the 283, but Impalas were usually ordered with the new 250-bhp 348-cid engine described earlier (see Chapter II). The Power-Pack option raised output to 280 bhp via three dual-throat carburetors with progressive linkage, dual exhausts, and 9.5:1 compression cylinder heads. Underneath was a much stronger X-type frame, with coil springs front and rear or optional air suspension. The latter proved unreliable due mainly to air leaks, and was quite expensive; few were sold. But the Impala itself proved so attractive that in 1959 it was made a separate series, the new top of the line.

Impala name was first seen on this 1956 Motorama showpiece. Windshield shape anticipated that of the '59 Chevy.

Despite the de-emphasis on performance caused partly by the AMA edict, the 280-bhp Impala was faster than the previous year's 270-bhp Bel Air. *Motor Trend* magazine found its Powerglide/Positraction-equipped hardtop would leap to 60 mph in 9.1 seconds and flash through the standing quarter mile in 16.5 seconds at 83.5 mph—no mean performance. "The Impala should easily win acceptance from the sports-minded automobile enthusiast. It's a solid car, with good cornering characteristics, plenty of power, and a chassis that should hold up under a rugged life."

The body-sharing 1959 Impala, like the whole

Chevrolet line, acquired the now-notorious "batwing" tailfin styling that was thought to be what the public wanted at the time. In fact, the fin fad was already on the way out. According to Carl Renner, the '59 might have been even worse. He recalls an early front-end proposal "which was a center theme with double headlights, one over other. It was a motif like the Edsel's central grille or the Tucker's third headlight... fortunately they did not come out with it" (doubly fortunate considering the fate of the Edsel and Tucker).

The 1959s offered still more potent engines, with up

1958 Impala Sport Coupe

1958 Bel Air Sport Sedan

1958 Impala convertible

Four-door sedan was a new Impala style for '59.

"Batwing" fins hurt sales of the long-lower-wider 1959 Chevys. Shown is the Biscayne two-door sedan.

to 315 horsepower. Air suspension was still available, though not much talked about, and would be dropped for 1960. But the big, curved fins (falsely rumored to lift the rear end off the ground at high speed) and a massively wide deck (Tom McCahill: "Enough room to land a Piper Cub") were detriments to really good sales. Ford soundly beat Chevy in 1959, by about 100,000 units.

Refinement (or retrenchment, depending on your viewpoint) was the word for 1960. Styling was much less radical as the wild tailfins were considerably toned down. "Probably the biggest difference between a 1960 Chevrolet and the previous model is the fact that it is much quieter when you drive it," noted *Motor Trend*. GM engineers had spent great effort on soundproofing and chassis refinements to make their cars more comfortable and silent.

The luxurious Impala remained much as it had been. Four-door models had been added for '59, and the convertible, two-door hardtop, four-door sedan, and four-door hardtop were all carried over for '60. As before, Chevrolet offered two V-8s and the 235.5-cid six, but various equipment options gave the buyer a choice of seven different power ratings. The performance-minded purchased their Impalas with the 348 V-8. It delivered 250 bhp in standard form, but there were four-barrel and triple-two-barrel carb options, with or without a special high-lift cam. The hottest combination was "three-twos with a cam," which delivered a tremendous 335 horsepower. Anyone who thought the 348 was a step backward from the "classic" 283 probably had their minds changed at traffic lights.

Chevy's 1960 chassis refinements should be mentioned, because they reflected the basic Impala concept that was evolving, one that would be continued all the way to the downsized models of 1977. A lower floor required a redesigned frame, with one new crossmember forward of the rear axle to anchor the upper control arm and add stiffness. Rear

coil springs were replaced by leaf springs, with a sway bar to help control rear-end roll. Body and engine mounts were redesigned, and employed new materials in a successful attempt to better isolate the body from vibration transmitted through the frame. Nylon sleeves covered shock absorber pistons, giving better hydraulic control of spring action.

The 1960 braking system employed larger-diameter front wheel cylinders to better equalize front/rear braking effort. Chevrolet also revised its parking brake but retained pedal actuation. If parking brake adjustment was off, a second touch on the pedal would assure complete application.

After concentrating heavily on mechanical modifications for 1960, Chevrolet made 1961 a

Styling was tamer for 1960, as this ragtop Impala shows.

1960 Impala Sport Sedan: smoother cruiser

Impala Sport Coupe displayed a cleaner look for 1961.

stylist's year. The esoteric tailfins were lost, which made the all-new cars dramatically cleaner and right up to date. These were the first Chevys to show the hand of Bill Mitchell, who had relieved Harley Earl as GM Styling chief in 1958. Mitchell's direction was responsible for an entirely new greenhouse, with larger glass area and very slim A- and C-pillars. The dogleg A-pillar with wraparound windshield, a Chevy feature since 1955, was eliminated. Mitchell also drastically altered the front and rear. The back end was notable for what *Motor Trend* called "a more gentle and refreshing rounded appearance over the harsh, flattened fin effect of 1960." The front end bore a passing resemblance to the 1960 look, but was neater. Altogether, this was the most pleasingly styled Chevy since 1955, and proved extremely popular. Over 1.2 million of the full-size '61s were sold, and the Impala accounted for 491,000 of them.

In January 1961, Chevrolet unofficially renounced the 1957 AMA decision against hot cars by introducing the first of the Super Sports. Technically a package option available on any model, the SS brought with it the first of the great 409-cid V-8s (see Chapter VII). Actually, there were three engine choices for the SS: the 409, and two 348s with 305 bhp (9.5:1 compression and four-barrel carb) or 364 bhp (11.25:1 compression and three two-barrels). But the 409 was *the* engine. A road test in late 1961 of a car

pulling an ultra-short 4.56:1 rear axle ratio produced an astounding standing-start quarter mile of 14 seconds at 98 mph and a 0–60 mph time of seven seconds flat. This, of course, was real street-racer stuff. More tractable and versatile was the 3.36:1 ratio, which gave slightly longer acceleration times, but a top speed that sent the Impala's 120-mph speedometer off the scale. The SS was a tremendous step forward for Chevy performance, and after 1961 the Division never looked back.

Almost immediately, Super Sports began to appear in competition around the country. Don Nicholson won the Stock Eliminator trophy at the 1961 NHRA Winternationals with his "dyno-tuned" SS409. His quarter-mile time was 13.59 seconds, his speed an astonishing 105.88 mph. North Carolinian Ned Jarrett became the NASCAR Grand National champion in another SS, and Dan Gurney even entered one in the production sedan class for Britain's International Trophy Race at Silverstone. Regrettably, the 409 had not yet been homologated by the Fédération Internationale de l'Automobile (FIA), so the SS was banned. It would have laid waste to the field had Gurney run.

"Street" Super Sport Impalas were lavishly outfitted. The interior sported a passenger grab bar, a floorshift trim plate on four-speed-equipped cars, a 7000-rpm tachometer, and SS emblems. The exterior was adorned with discreet SS badges, triple-spinner wheelcovers, and 8.00×14 narrow-band whitewalls. Standard spec also called for heavy-duty springs and shocks, sintered metallic brake linings, power brakes, and power steering. SS equipment was usually ordered on Impalas, and virtually all were two-door hardtops, though a few '61 convertibles were also built. A handful of Bel Air hardtops may also have been given the SS treatment.

Chevy performance was back!

Impala Super Sport arrived in mid-1961, sported special emblems, tunnel shift plate, and column-mounted tach.

1962-66 Corvair Spyder/Corsa:

The Terrific Turbos

Special dash, decklid emblem, and protruding exhaust set Spyder apart from lesser Corvairs. Shown is the '64 convertible.

If Chevy hadn't conceived the Corvair Monza Spyder, some other carmarker surely would have. By the early '60s, the reliability and performance inherent in Dr. Ferdinand Porsche's concept of a rear-mounted, air-cooled engine powering a sleek, lightweight car riding an all-independent suspension had been solidly proven. For many sports car enthusiasts, that formula was the "state of the art" and the way of the future. For them, Porsche was the most sophisticated production sports car in the world. How many would have believed that Chevrolet was about to offer something along the same lines for roughly half the price?

The only thing wrong with a super-hot, turbocharged Corvair was that the basic product wasn't selling too well. The rear-engine concept, which the original Corvair of 1960 pioneered among mass-production U.S. cars, was failing dismally in the sales wars against the utterly conventional Ford Falcon. And it would be lack of volume—not Ralph Nader—that would ultimately spell the end of the Corvair. The decision to drop the car after tooling costs for the revised 1965 line had been amortized was made six months before Nader's *Unsafe at Any Speed* was published.

The Monza Spyder of 1962–64 (and its Corsa successor of 1965–66) was created in response to what GM saw as an unexpected market for Corvairs: young people who wanted something sporty, rather than middle-aged people who wanted mainly economy. It was felt that the Chevy II and Chevelle could cater to the average buyer, while the Corvair could become more specialized. Unfortunately, Ford's Mustang, with its cheaper components and a plethora of options, buried the Corvair during 1964–65, causing Chevrolet managers to opt for the Mustang-like Camaro.

Turbocharging was an obvious way to make Corvairs faster, and different types of units had been tried on the "pancake" six before Chevy's. Paxton, for example, had offered its SN-60 centrifugal blower as an aftermarket item priced at $365. That device enabled Paxton's Andy Granatelli to reach 142 mph at the Bonneville Salt Flats. Chevy even used the Paxton unit on its Corvair Sebring Spyder SS showcar of 1961. So, GM decided that the turbocharger was the best way to hot rod the production model. The engineering work was handled by J. O. Brafford and R. E. Threson.

As most enthusiasts know, turbocharging works much like a windmill in principle. The "wind" in this case is exhaust gases that spin a turbine wheel or impeller. Power is transferred by a shaft connected to another impeller, which spins the compressor. This squeezes or pressurizes fuel and air into a very dense mixture. As the rate of exhaust flow increases and temperature rises, the compressor turbine spins faster and faster, creating positive pressure ("boost") in the manifold.

The Corvair turbocharger was manufactured to a Chevy design by Thompson Valve Division of

Thompson-Ramo-Wooldridge (now TRW) Inc. It had an 11-blade impeller cast integrally with a half-inch shaft, and enclosed in a snail-shaped housing. Exhaust gases flowed inward from the outer edge of the housing and exited at the side. A 14-blade die-cast compressor was bolted to the other end of the shaft, and pressurized the fuel/air mixture outwards from the entrance point. The turbo weighed only 13.5 pounds, and was mounted slightly off center in the forward part of the engine compartment to leave room for heater ducting. A third aluminum housing separated these two components, and contained a floating bearing for the shaft. Exhaust flow was carried through the stock twin manifolds via a lower crossover pipe mounted ahead of the engine, then up and into the turbine chamber. A cast iron heat shield protected the bearing housing and compressor end of the turbo. Carburetion was conventional: a Carter type YH sidedraft unit with three concentric venturis. The carb was dressed up with chrome bolt heads and linkages set against a glossy, black-finished body.

Due to the increased stresses associated with turbocharging, Spyder engines were beefed up with super-strength materials for many internal components, such as chrome steel for the crankshaft. Connecting rod column width was increased, and piston rings were made of high-strength centrifugal cast iron. The valvetrain from the normally aspirated 98-horsepower engine was retained, but exhaust valve heads were made of "Nomonic 80A" super alloy (largely nickel and chrome), an exotic material needed to withstand exhaust valve temperatures some 200 degrees higher than normal. To help protect the powerplant in sustained high-rpm running, GM engineers also fitted a temperature gauge in the lefthand cylinder head, plus a snap switch at the number one combustion chamber hooked to a warning light and buzzer. Spyders also had an eight-plate oil cooler instead of the three-plate unit used on unblown models.

The turbocharged Corvair engine produced 150 bhp at 4400 rpm—over one bhp per cubic inch, and 52 bhp more than the stock unit. Torque was similarly improved: 210 pounds-feet at 3200–3400 rpm, up 64 percent. The turbo engine was undoubtedly the most exotic production Corvair powerplant, and was very advanced by the standards of the early '60s.

The Monza Spyder made its debut in February 1962, but as volume production didn't begin until April, availability was limited. Only 6894 were built, 2574 of them convertibles. The Spyder package was listed as RPO 690, priced at a reasonable $317.45, and included heavy-duty suspension. Orders far exceeded capacity that year, much buyer enthusiasm involving aspects of the car other than its fine performance.

A Monza Spyder was the kind of car the aficionado could tell at a glance, though the casual observer might not notice anything unusual. Only a 2.5-inch chrome tailpipe protruding from a special outlet in the

The Spyder's turbo engine: 150 bhp from 145 cid.

Convertible was new for 1962. Just 7472 of these '63 Monza Spyder ragtops were built.

Spyder was an equipment option for 1962-63 Monzas (1963 convertible shown), became separate model for '64.

rear pan and a small, die-cast emblem attached to the rear deck gave the game away externally. Flip up the engine cover, however, and you'd see lots of chrome-plated parts not found on lesser models: crossover pipe, oil lines, fuel lines, dipstick handle, and exhaust shield.

More differences were evident in the cockpit. The plain-looking Corvair instrument cluster was replaced by one covered by a brushed aluminum appliqué and housing a complete set of businesslike dials: 6000-rpm tachometer, 120-mph speedometer, and smaller gauges for manifold pressure, engine temperature, and fuel level. Brushed aluminum also graced the central radio panel and passenger-side

Spyder's discreet fender script (left) and beautiful brushed-aluminum dash with full instrumentation (right)

glovebox door. This beautiful dash was quite popular, and many were pirated in later years by builders of Corvair beach buggies.

Despite a 13-percent drop in Corvair production for 1963, Spyder output was up as Chevy raced to fill backlog orders. Some 19,099 were built, of which 7472 were convertibles. Mechanical revisions included a hotter cam, standard PCV valve, and removal of the throttle-return check valve. At mid-year, engine compartment finish was changed from exterior body color to gloss black. Cosmetic and equipment touches shared with other Corvairs were a fully transistorized radio, self-adjusting brakes, new front and rear exterior trim, restyled hubcaps, revised upholstery, improved door locks, and the use of exhaust valve rotators to cut down on valve wear.

Spyder production fell to 11,241 for the 1964 model year, convertibles accounting for 4761 of them. To the delight of those who loved the cars, prices remained stable—the base figure was never higher than $2800. For the first time, the Spyder was listed as a separate model instead of a sub-series in the Monza line. Wheel

covers were now unique, bearing the image of a gold spider in their centers.

Mechanical alterations for '64 included a chrome-plated air cleaner and a return to the 1962 camshaft profile. Spyders also received a 12-plate oil cooler and larger-diameter clutch disc. Greater displacement—up from 145 cubic inches to 164 cid—was achieved by lengthening stroke from 2.60 to 2.94 inches. Predictably, torque was up, though horsepower remained at 150. Both the three- and four-speed manual transmissions were revised with closer ratios and heavier synchros. Though the three-speed was theoretically available, most Spyders were equipped with the four-speed unit.

Probably the most interesting 1964 option was Kelsey-Hayes wire wheels, supplied to Chevy with special adaptors, nuts, and even a rubber hammer for the "knock-off" hubs. These wheels are extremely rare today, since only 400 or 500 Corvairs were so equipped. Fewer still, of course, found their way onto Monza Spyders. The wires would have been more common had K-H marketed them independently, but

Note front-end trim differences between the 1963 Spyder convertible (above) and the two '64s (below).

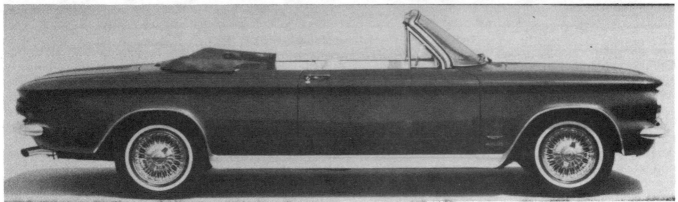

Factory photo of the 1964 Monza Spyder shows rare Kelsey-Hayes wire wheel option.

the firm sold its entire 1962 production to Chevrolet. The price was $400 at that time; today, collectors pay up to twice that much for a prime set.

Distinguishing the various first-generation turbo 'Vairs is easiest from the front. The '62s used twin, black, horizontal dummy grilles with horizontal wind-splits; the '63s had a full-width horizontal strip with black center; the '64s retained the black insert, but added a center emblem in the shape of an inverted triangle.

The second-generation 1965–69 Corvair was developed in 1962 at the height of the rear-engine Chevy's success, and Bill Mitchell's staff put everything they had into it. The result was one of the most timelessly beautiful cars in history. Generations from now, it will rank with the 1956 Continental Mark II, 1953–54 Studebaker coupes, and the 1963 Corvette Sting Ray among the all-time great automotive designs. Indeed, it looked more Italian than American. Perfectly contoured, exciting from every angle, never overstated, this new Corvair was a solid sales . . . flop. It was simply uncompetitive with Ford's equally new Mustang, which was destined to start a craze for something that would be named in its honor—the "ponycar." But for those who appreciate it, the second-generation Corvair is a very desirable automobile, particularly the turbocharged models. They are perhaps the most outstanding cars in the Corvair's entire 10-year production life.

Offered only for 1965–66, the Corsa was now the top of the line. It was the successor to the Spyder, though factory photos show that Chevy changed the name only at the last minute. Both hardtop ($2500) and convertible ($2700) body styles were available. The blown engine, now developing 180 bhp, was optional for Corsa, the standard powerplant being a special four-carburetor 140-bhp non-turbo unit. All Corsas were delivered with complete instrumentation and deluxe interior at no extra charge. Production was 20,291 coupes and 8353 convertibles for 1965, followed by 7330 coupes and 3142 convertibles for '66. Though the Corvair continued for 1967–69, the Corsa was dropped to make room for the new Camaro

and to hold down production costs while the dies were run out.

In turbocharged form, the 1965–66 Corsas were quicker than the Spyders. Typical 0–60 mph acceleration was 9.5 seconds, and the car could hit 115 mph given enough room. Yet gas mileage was still over 20 mpg at rational speeds on the highway.

Getting 180 bhp out of the blown engine for '65 was not too difficult, because the Corvair engine had been relatively unstressed. To do it, Chevy introduced new cylinder heads with larger valves and ports. The head and cam design duplicated those of the Monza Spyder, but the turbocharger had wider impeller blades for increased air flow and pressure output.

A total of 80,000 Monza Spyders and Corsas were produced. Many of them would be owned for lengthy periods by people for whom they never lost their appeal. Despite their relatively low volume, these cars spawned a variety of aftermarket accessories. Dick

Corsa replaced Spyder as the top Corvair for 1965.

The 1966 Corsa coupe: beautiful from any angle.

Griffin, for example, famous for his Corvair drag racers, developed a special aluminum manifold that would accept a Stromberg WW carburetor. For those who wanted aluminum-bronze valve guides, EMPI in California could oblige, even if Chevrolet wouldn't. Most Corvair enthusiasts today wouldn't "wrap" an exhaust system on a bet, but this was a popular way of improving performance in the '60s. It increased exhaust temperature, making the gases move faster for higher turbine speeds—at the expense of decreased life for the crossover pipes. Another non-stock means of boosting horsepower was water injection (seen briefly in production on Oldsmobile's turbocharged F-85 Jetfire of 1962–63), and was also available on the aftermarket. Usually sold in kit form, it included water tanks to be mounted in the engine compartment. And for $150 your Spyder or blown Corsa could be equipped with Bill Thomas' "SS" setup: two carburetors plus a larger induction tube. With these, the existing turbo pressurized through the carbs instead of drawing its mixture from the stock Carter unit. Thomas claimed another 40 horses.

We've seen the end of modified Corvairs now. By the late '70s, it had become very difficult to find good original Spyders and Corsas, and many had regrettably been turned into beach buggies. Today, collector prices for these cars are rapidly moving upward. Yet, apart from rebuilding the blower, turbo 'Vairs aren't expensive or difficult to restore or maintain, and the blower rebuild really isn't as hard as it might appear.

Nowadays, Corvair Monza Spyders and Corsas, blown and unblown, are being recognized as the fine automobiles they were, now that the tide of misinformation unleashed by the Nader book is subsiding. Despite Chevrolet's lackluster support and the many ill-bred rumors surrounding the Corvair, these two models really provided a preview of the 1980s. Today, turbocharging has become an increasingly common solution to the problem of resolving the conflict between performance, tight emission controls, and fuel economy mandates. Though the air-cooled rear-mounted engine concept has given way even at Porsche, today's turbo cars owe much to Spyder/Corsa technology. In that respect, at least, the Corvair truly was a wave of the future. Perhaps that makes these most sophisticated of performance Chevys from the '60s the most contemporary of collector cars for the '80s.

Low production, high performance, and timeless styling make Corsa (1966 shown) a desireable collector's item today.

One of just 3142 Corsa convertibles built for 1966. The companion coupes numbered just 7330 that year.

Milestone Engines/II

409, 396, 427, 400, and 454 V-8s

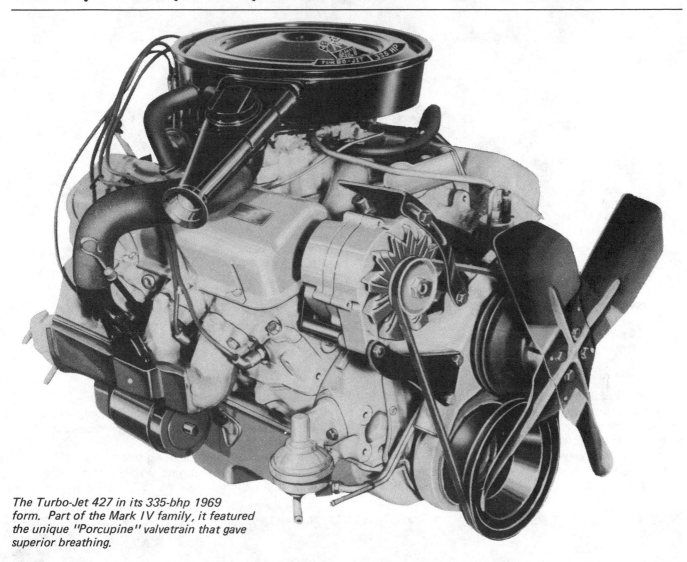

The Turbo-Jet 427 in its 335-bhp 1969 form. Part of the Mark IV family, it featured the unique "Porcupine" valvetrain that gave superior breathing.

Four-Oh-Nine! From its burbling throb at idle to its high-rpm scream, Chevy's 409 cubic-inch V-8 was a sensation. What was the magic in this new engine? Was it just cubic inches? Well, it was that, plus something else—that indefinable quality an engine has when everything in it is designed to match everything else.

The 409's magical power was evident almost from the day it appeared in 1961. For example, Dan Gurney tore around Riverside in a stock 409 Impala to beat Dave McDonald's lap record, which had been set with the hottest, fuel-injected 283 Corvette. Gurney raced his car in England that same year—but only once. He led the race, outpacing a pack of tuned 3.8-liter (232 cubic-inch) twin-cam Jaguar sedans, until his Chevy lost a wheel. But the 409 had been fast enough to make its mark on the European scene. It went on to a career in NASCAR oval-track events, and was a surprise winner at the 1961 NHRA Winternationals, where Don Nicholson's Impala was timed over the standing-start quarter mile at 13.19 seconds at nearly 110 mph. Thus began what would become a legend in Chevy performance history.

Actually, there had been a big-block V-8 before the 409. It was the type W, the most unlikely starting point for a big-inch powerhouse imaginable. To understand

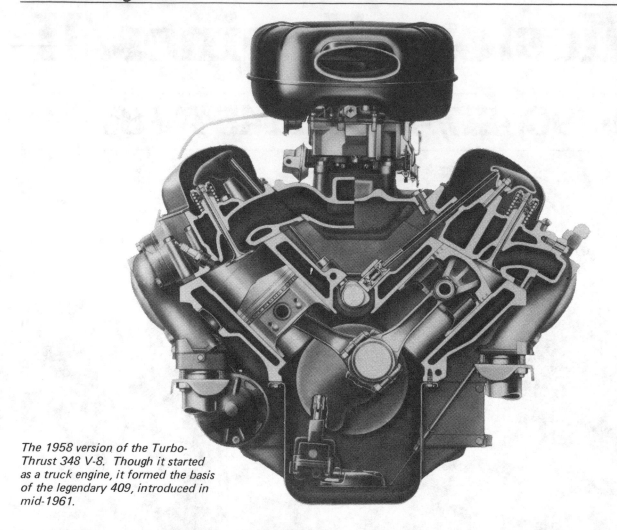

The 1958 version of the Turbo-Thrust 348 V-8. Though it started as a truck engine, it formed the basis of the legendary 409, introduced in mid-1961.

how the 409 came to be, you have to go back to 1958.

Chevy's 283-cid V-8 was hardly a year old when engineers discovered—to their great dismay—that it wouldn't be able to provide competitive performance for the larger, heavier models planned for 1958 and beyond. Chevy was going to need a lot more cubes in a hurry, way beyond the 302 that was the limit for that

block and then-current crankshaft. Almost in desperation, they looked to the only bigger V-8 they had, a new 348-cid mill—wincing a little, because it was primarily intended for trucks. But there was nothing else to use as a starting point for a high-performance car engine, so the type W it was.

With its 4.125-inch bore and 3.25-inch stroke in a

The advent of larger, heavier Chevys in the late '50s (1958 Impala shown) led to development of the 348 V-8.

block having cylinder center-to-center spacing of 4.84 inches, the 348 had plenty of room for enlargement. For car applications it was given the name "Turbo-Thrust" to distinguish it from the small-block V-8s, which were named "Turbo-Fire." It was designed by John T. Rausch as project leader, with Howard Kehrl and Donald McPherson working as his principal assistants.

Hotting up the 348 began in mid-1958. There were new and wilder camming, multi-carburetor setups, compression ratios that would have made Kettering proud, and many other little tricks to gain efficiency without losing reliability. This work was handled by Maurice Rosenberger, an ex-Cadillac engine man, assisted by Fred Frincke and Dennis Davis. After developing satisfactory 348s for both racing and street use, this team turned to developing an enlargement, which became the 409.

In concept, the 409 was supposed to be simply a bored-out 348 with a longer stroke. The production unit, however, ended up having only a few inter-changeable parts. Cylinder blocks and heads for both engines were machined on the same lines, though, which was a vital bit of help from the cost angle. In boring out the 348 block, Chevy carefully avoided any changes in the casting. For one thing, it was considered imperative to retain the full-circle water jackets around the bores. This limited the maximum bore increase to $^3/_{16}$-inch (0.1875-inch), giving a final bore dimension of 4.3125 inches. Stroke was increased from 3.25 to 3.50 inches, which called for a new crankshaft. Both the 348 and 409 had forged-steel crankshafts, though the latter had longer crank throws. Bearing sizes were also shared—2.50-inch diameter for the mains and 2.20-inch diameter for the crankpins. The 409's crank demanded heavier counterweights, however, and consequently weighed 8.2 pounds more for a total of 67 pounds.

To keep the same deck height, it became necessary to shorten the connecting rods. This had the drawback of increasing maximum rod angularity and therefore, side thrust on the piston. While the 348 had permanent-mold cast-aluminum pistons, the 409 was fitted with forged-aluminum pistons for greater heat resistance. The 348 employed offset piston pins, which had the benefit of reducing piston-skirt slap after a cold start. That makes a truck engine more civilized, but has no real importance for a high-performance car. The 409, however, had no piston-pin offset, so there was no need for separate lefts and rights. In the 348, valve relief cavities were on opposite sides of the topland. The 409 pistons had milled valve reliefs, all on the same side.

Like the entire basic layout, the valve gear design for the 348 was taken from the small-block engine. This meant ballstud-mounted, stamped-steel rocker arms and valves arranged in line at a 12-degree inclination above wedge-shaped combustion chambers. Cylinder heads for both the 348 and 409 were made from the

same castings, but the 409 had wider pushrod holes and different valve-spring abutment faces. It also had stronger valve springs than the 348 for sure closing at high rpm, as well as stronger, thicker pushrods. The 409 used a single coil spring with a flat steel damper per valve, while the 348 had dual valve springs. Both intake and exhaust valves on the 409 were inherited from the 348, the intakes measuring 2.066 inches across the head and the exhausts 1.72 inches.

As a reworked 348, the 409 naturally featured higher compression (11.25:1) and a wilder camshaft. Intake-valve lift was raised from 0.406 to 0.440-inch, and exhaust-valve lift from 0.412 to the same 0.440. Intake-valve opening duration was extended from 287 to 317 degrees, and overlap (the period during which both valves are open) from 66 to 70 degrees.

In 1960 the 348 had been offered with a triple two-barrel carburetor setup that boosted rated power from 340 to 350 bhp. No multi-carburetor manifolds were devised for the initial version of the 409, because its big four-barrel Carter had almost the same airflow volume as the three deuces.

The 409 debuted as a mid-1961 option. In its most powerful form it delivered 360 bhp at 5800 rpm, and generated peak torque of 409 pounds-feet at 3600 rpm. It weighed 664 pounds, only 34 pounds more than the 230 cubic-inch Chevrolet six. A 409-bhp option with dual four-barrels by Carter became available for 1962. The following year, a full 425 bhp was claimed for this combination, thanks to an 11.0:1 compression ratio and solid lifters. The same engine with a single four-barrel Carter was rated at 400 bhp. The twin four-barrel option was discontinued at the end of the 1964 model year. For 1965, the hottest 409 was rated at 400 bhp. It sported a big-port aluminum intake manifold, 11.0:1 compression ratio, a high-lift/high-overlap camshaft with solid lifters, single four-barrel carburetor, and special low-resistance exhaust manifolds. A 340-bhp version was carried over unchanged from '64, with 10.0:1 compression, single four-barrel carb, and hydraulic lifters.

Early in 1963, a mysterious new Chevrolet 427 V-8 appeared at Daytona International Speedway. After being shocked by its acceleration and speed, rivals who were able to look at it with the rocker covers off noticed its odd valve angles, and nicknamed it the "Porcupine" engine. In the 500-mile race, the Chevy simply sped away, leaving all other cars behind, and lapped at average speeds up to 166 mph before dropping out—due to unspecified engine failure. Shortly after that, GM's top management put a ban on racing activities by its car divisions, and no more was heard of the "Porcupine." However, development work on it continued unabated at the GM Technical Center in Warren, Michigan. It resurfaced in the spring of 1965 as a high-performance option for the Chevelle, the full-size Chevrolet, and the Corvette, with capacity cut to 396 cid.

Design and development work on the "Porcupine" is

credited to a team consisting of Richard L. Keinath, assistant staff engineer; Herbert G. Sood, project engineer; and William J. Polkinghorne. Keinath had helped Don McPherson design the four- and six-cylinder Chevy II engines in 1960–61, and had been working on V-8 projects since then. He had joined General Motors in 1950, arriving at Chevrolet in 1956. However, the idea for the "Porcupine" valvetrain and overall engine design came from Robert P. Benzinger, who had laid out and detailed the all-aluminum Corvair flat six, and was gaining recognition among Chevrolet's technical staff as the Division's top engine man.

What was new and unusual about the valve gear was that it resulted from working "backwards." Normally, an engine designer starts with the combustion chambers, and arranges the valves so they can be operated by simple, straightforward mechanisms. Benzinger felt that better results could be obtained by giving attention to breathing rather than just locating mechanical parts. Accordingly, he started with the ports and manifolds, giving them ideal dimensions and

gas flow paths, and left the valves till later. Valves are happy enough working at almost any angle, but what about the pushrods? They can't be bent, but must go straight from the lifter to the rocker arm. With very few compromises, Benzinger poked the pushrods through little openings to the oddest places—and the whole thing worked superbly well.

Intake valves were set at an angle of 26 degrees to the cylinder axis, and exhaust valves were tilted 17 degrees from the same axis. That wasn't all, for both intake and exhaust valve stems were also tilted in side view, one forwards and the other backwards, by 9 degrees. This lined them up with the pushrods to avoid setting up any rotation in the rocker arms. This basic cylinder-head configuration was then tested, fiddled with, honed, and polished until it provided optimal breathing. That part of the design was then frozen, and all other components were designed around it.

The 396 V-8 was just one member of a whole "Porcupine" family, officially titled Mark IV and marketed as the "Turbo-Jet." There were four in all:

1966 Chevelle SS396 was a real stormer. Chevy's midsize was totally restyled. Note hardtop's "tunnelback" roof.

All Chevelle Super Sports became SS396s for 1966. Output this year was 325 and 360 bhp.

two high-performance car engines of 396 and 427 cid, a 366 cid heavy-duty truck unit, and a 427 heavy-duty marine version. The 396 was scheduled to replace the 409 in all its applications, even though that engine was hardly old. Why was it scrapped after barely five years' production? Aside from its basic design limitations, the type W had been tooled for relatively low production volume. To meet future demands, Chevy's Tonawanda, New York, plant (near Niagara) would have to be retooled anyway. Semon E. "Bunkie" Knudsen, then division general manager, decided that only the most modern engine could justify such a major tooling reinvestment, so the "Porcupine" got the nod.

There was no thought of any carryover from the type W or 409 to the Mark IV. An all-new block with 4.84-inch spacing between bore centers was chosen, giving a bore of 4.094 inches. Stroke was 3.76 inches.

The 409 block had a deck angled at 33 degrees from horizontal to allow a wedge-shaped combustion chamber to be created with flat-faced heads. By contrast, the Mark IV block had the usual deck angle of 45 degrees to the cylinder axis. Main bearings were 2.75 inches in diameter, a quarter-inch larger than in the type W. Main-bearing width was also increased, adding two full inches to the cap-clamping surface. The forged-steel crankshaft was cross-drilled to deliver oil to the rod bearings through a full 360 degrees of rotation (a feature the W lacked), and crankpin journals were kept at 2.20-inch diameter.

The 396 was initially offered in two versions, both with four-barrel carburetors, 10.25:1 compression, and hydraulic lifters. One was rated at 325 bhp, the other at 360. Production began at mid-year 1965 at the Tonawanda plant where all Mark IVs were built. There was also a 425-bhp version listed as a Corvette option that year. It had 11.0:1 compression, impact-extruded alloy pistons with chrome-plated rings, solid lifters, bigger carburetors with twin-snorkel air cleaner, and enlarged oil pan capacity. This engine was in very short supply, but it wasn't short on performance. With it, a car geared for a top speed of 140 mph could blast

Big Impala SS adopted a rounder look for 1967. Big 427 V-8 was more widely available than in '66.

Impala SS was still available with a lowly six in '67. Just 9545 convertibles were built that year.

through the standing-start quarter mile in 14 seconds flat at a terminal speed of 102–104 mph.

For 1966, the 396 was superseded by the 427, which had the same stroke but was bored out to 4.251 inches. It became more widely available for the Corvette and full-size Chevrolet in 1967. There were 390- and 425-bhp versions, the latter having enlarged valves, 11.0:1 compression, and solid lifters.

During 1967, Chevrolet brought out its L-88 option for the 427. This included aluminum cylinder heads with enlarged ports, a hotter camshaft, and bigger carburetor. The aluminum heads reduced engine weight from 687 pounds to near the 327's 575 pounds. Equipped with a big four-barrel Holley, solid lifters, and 11.25:1 compression ratio, the L-88 was rated at a mighty 450 bhp. In the Chevelle SS, it could deliver standing-start quarter-mile times of under 15 seconds at terminal velocities of around 100 mph. That was too close to the Ram-Air 400 GTO for Pontiac's comfort, and its performance fiends soon began stuffing a 455 V-8 into that car. Chevrolet would

also go the route of adding extra cubic inches in short order.

Not that the technical brains weren't trying to pump more power out of the smaller engines. As early as 1961, Corvette wizard Zora Arkus-Duntov had tested a 327 with overhead cams and three valves per cylinder. And that wasn't all: there was a 427 V-8 on test in 1967 with one overhead camshaft per bank and electronic fuel injection. Duntov told *Hot Rod* magazine in 1967: "We've seen well over 600 horsepower out of some of our big-block experimentation."

For the 1970 model year, Chevrolet announced a 454-cid expansion of the Mark IV, available for Monte Carlo, Chevelle, the big Chevrolet, and Corvette. At the same time, two 400-cid engines appeared on the specs charts, but they were totally different. One was actually a slightly larger 402 derivative of the big-block 396. The other was a small-block unit based on the thick-web 350 that was a direct descendant of the fabled 327.

Chevy engineers had to bend some of their rules to

For 1967, the big-block Mark IV was bored out to 427 cid. This is the 390-horse version; 425 bhp was also available.

get as much as 400 cubes from the small-block with its 4.40-inch bore spacing and short deck height. That configuration imposed a definite limit on how far stroke could be stretched without pulling the pistons too far out of their holes. Boring out to 4.125 inches left less than a quarter-inch between the bores, and that had to be solid metal, with no water jacketing to separate the cylinders. The 350's 3.48-inch stroke was extended to 3.75 inches, which necessitated larger-diameter (2.65 inches instead of 2.45) main bearings to assure adequate overlap between the mains and the crankpin journals. That, in turn, required a new, heftier, and heavier crankshaft. The longer stroke caused an increase in piston speed that aggravated the greater heat-sensitivity of the siamesed cylinders. As a result, the small-block Turbo-Fire 400 had no potential as a performance engine. It did have advantages for emissions control, however, because of its more favorable surface-to-volume ratio. The most Chevy ever got from it was a rated 265 bhp.

By contrast, the Turbo-Jet 400 belonged to the big-block Mark IV family. It had almost the same cylinder dimensions as the small-block unit (4.126 × 3.76 inches), but delivered a hefty 330 bhp on 10.25:1 compression for 1970. The 454 launched that same year was basically the Mark IV design, with stroke extended to a full 4.00 inches. It came in two forms: the 390-bhp LS-5, with hydraulic lifters, 10.25:1 compression, and a four-barrel Rochester carb; and the 460-bhp LS-7, with solid lifters, 11.25:1 compression, and four-barrel Holley, plus a special higher-lift camshaft and transistorized ignition.

The big-blocks were the culmination of Chevrolet's performance engine development. But these potent powerplants wouldn't take kindly to the anti-smog devices needed to meet stiffening emission standards beginning in 1973. That year, America would get its first "fuel shock," which ultimately would sentence big-inch high-performance cars to oblivion. Up to that time, Tonawanda was turning out 300,000 Mark IV V-8s annually. By the end of the 1976 model year, the big-block engine family would be gone.

The first 454-cid Mark IV enlargement arrived for 1970. Shown is the 460-bhp LS-7 unit with 3x2 carbs.

1962-67 Impala SS:

The Smooth, Spacious Sizzler

From 1961 through 1969, Chevrolet produced some of the most blindingly fast full-size cars in the world. Though Impala Super Sports went mostly unrecognized until a few years ago, there is growing interest in these cars today. This partly reflects the enormous price escalation among 1955–57 Chevys, but it also shows that the very special character of the big SS is beginning to be appreciated on its own merits. Not every SS was a big-block bruiser, of course. In most years you could buy one with a mild-mannered six. But the ones being gathered up today are of the hairier variety—and in a class by themselves. In the '60s, too, they were "top of the line" for many Chevy fans.

Origins of the SS go back to the mighty 409 V-8 (see Chapter VII). The Super Sport package arrived as a mid-1961 offering, and was partly devised to complement that engine. Still, there would never have been an SS—with or without the 409—had there not first been a Corvair Monza. That was the car which proved to Detroit that bucket seats, floorshifts, and luxury interiors would turn on a great many buyers the industry had never tried to reach before. If buckets and floorshifts helped sell Corvairs, why wouldn't they help sell the big Chevys, too? This, and not the 409, was the business rationale for the SS. Fortunately, the people who designed it liked automobiles, and they gave us something great.

In addition to the 409 (or any one of three 348-cid V-8s ranging from 305 to 350 horsepower), here's what purchasers of Super Sport "kits" got for their

money in 1961: special spinner wheel covers gracing 8.00 × 14 narrow-band whitewalls, dashboard grab bar, padded dash, transmission tunnel trim plate (with four-speed floorshift), column-mounted 7000-rpm tach, heavy-duty springs and shocks, sintered metallic brake linings, power brakes and steering, and SS emblems on fenders, dash, and rear deck. The package was technically available on any Impala including two-door sedans and four-door sedans and hardtops, but virtually all Super Sports actually built were convertibles or two-door hardtops. A variety of rear axle ratios was available so buyers could tailor the car to their individual needs. With the 4.56:1 gearing, for example, you had a 14-second/100-mph quarter-mile drag racer. With the 3.36:1 ratio, you might do the quarter in 15 seconds, but your top speed bordered on 140 mph.

With only 453 SS cars built for 1961, Chevy was barely testing the waters. But the waters looked promising, so the Division plunged in for 1962. Besides the big-blocks, the SS could now be equipped with any engine found in the plain Impala, right down to the 135-bhp six. Again, most buyers insisted on a romping, stomping 409 with 380 or 409 bhp, or at least a 327 (replacing the 348 that year) with 250 or 300 horses. Chevy went out of its way to make the '62s more readily identifiable as Super Sports than the '61s. There were anodized-aluminum body moldings and rear deck "cove" inserts, special "SS" badges on the sides and deck, and wheel covers with simulated knock-off hubs. Inside were center console, standard bucket seats edged with bright aluminum trim, more aluminum trim on the instrument panel, plus the passenger-side grab bar. These easily adaptable decorations and accessories largely stayed with the SS through its remaining eight years of production.

Though there was nothing to compare with the 409 for real power, the new 327 was so good that a lot of SS buyers chose it instead. More flexible than the 409, it had been developed from the legendary 283. In 300-bhp form it was equipped with a new and beefier crankshaft, stronger main and rod bearing inserts, and oversize ports and exhaust valves. The 327 gave tremendous mid-range performance and good off-the-mark dig, plus more refined highway behavior and improved fuel consumption compared with the 409. For fanciers of what the Europeans called "grand touring," a 300-bhp Impala SS327 would go a long way toward meeting their demand.

Special show interior on a '61 Impala SS

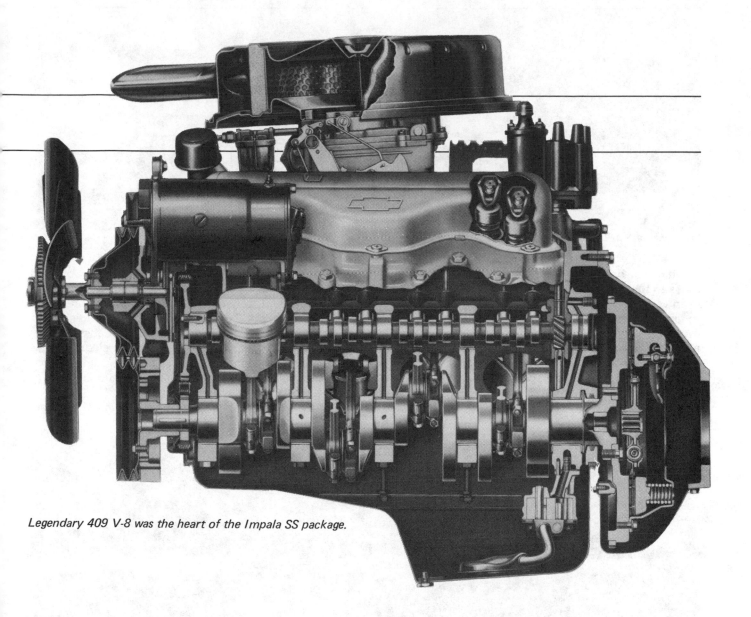

Legendary 409 V-8 was the heart of the Impala SS package.

Unfortunately, touring grandly was about all the SS did. Despite the best efforts of tuners like Smokey Yunick and drivers like Junior Johnson, the cars didn't shine on the NASCAR tracks. Pontiacs and Fords were more often the winners. Several stock eliminator trophies fell to Chevy in the drag-race sweepstakes, but this was the only bright spot in an otherwise bleak competition picture. A half-hearted racing assistance program and very determined efforts by Chevy's rivals were the main factors.

Several special competition engines were in the works for 1963–64, but were never fully developed due to corporate policy. A 427-cid version of the 409—the so-called "mystery" Z-11 Mark II, with an alleged 500-plus horsepower available in tuned form—was designed, but not fully tested. Few were built, and the best a Z-11 ever did was ninth place at the Daytona

500. After 1964, both Chevy and Pontiac backed away from racing. Thus, the SS remained a car of unexplored competition potential, even while it was attracting a host of fans who loved it for the smooth and spacious sizzler it was.

For 1963, the Super Sport could again be a sheep in wolf's clothing with the basic (140-bhp) six or 283-cid (195-bhp) V-8. From there you could go up to 250- and 300-bhp 327s, followed by three 409 engines ranging from 340 to 425 bhp. The 340 version, by the way, was no slouch. In a *Car Life* magazine road test, this engine teamed with the 3.36 axle and Powerglide gave 0–60 mph times of around 6.5 seconds and a top speed in the neighborhood of 125 mph.

At the other end of the scale, the 425-bhp 409 had special high-compression heads, oversize valves, and

Listed for any '63 Impala, SS option was fitted only to two-door hardtops (left) and convertibles (right).

two big four-barrel aluminum carburetors. It got 10 miles to the gallon, and went fast enough to scare even village hot rodders. Properly equipped—which meant the hardest suspension you could buy and metallic linings to help the brakes—the 425 was a mean machine indeed, certainly one of the most rapid automobiles Chevy ever turned out. And with gas in those days running at perhaps 30 cents for a gallon of 100-octane premium, nobody much complained about the mileage.

The boxy, razor-edge lines of the big Chevy softened for 1964 as the '61 bodyshell got its final facelift. The two-door hardtop's squared-off roof with its convertible-look "bow" creases was retained, but tinware below the belt was reworked with concave instead of convex creases. In all, the result was less elegant than the 1961–63 versions. The old body was beginning to show its age, and would be replaced by a brand-new one for 1965.

One interesting development for '64 was that the

Styling became more rounded for '64 Impala SS. The top 409 V-8 produced 425 bhp.

Subtle emblems, distinctive spinner wheel covers set SS apart from "family" Impalas. Shown is the '64 convertible.

Impala SS was made a separate series for 1964. Simulated convertible top "bows" marked the hardtop.

Impala SS was made a separate line distinct from the rank-and-file Impala. There were four basic models: hardtop coupe and convertible, six and V-8. Despite its new top-of-the-line status, the SS looked little different from other big Chevys apart from its bucket-seat interior, available in eight different color choices and amply decorated with SS emblems. Unfortunately, the dashboard was still the same know-nothing affair used on all the full-size models, distinguished only by a column-mounted tach.

While the '64 Super Sport engine lineup remained identical to that of 1963, enthusiastic shifters now had two different four-speeds to choose from. For all-around use, the well-known M20 gearbox offered decent flexibility with relatively high intermediate gearing. For the 400- and 425-bhp 409s only, the M21 close-ratio box was listed, and combined with 4.11 or 4.56 rear axle ratios to produce eye-popping acceleration. Although the rival Ford 427, Dodge 426, and Pontiac 421 were more than a match for the now-aging 409, the Super Sport was still a fine performance car, desired by many. About 185,000 Impala SS models were sold for '64, with hardtops outnumbering convertibles by about 5.5 to one.

The record sales year of 1965 saw Chevrolet and other GM divisions fully redesign their big cars—and sell them literally as fast as they came off the assembly line. The Impala SS reached its peak. Almost a quarter million were built, with V-8s vastly outnumbering sixes. The bulkier, more round styling featured "coke-bottle" rear fender contours, and was something of an improvement on the '64 look. The Impala SS remained one of the most attractive of the sporty big cars.

On the inside, the 1965 SS was much improved. Luxurious carpeting, color-keyed vinyl upholstery, and front bucket seats were retained, but full instrumentation was added, housed in large round dials on each side of the broad strip speedometer. The lefthand combination dial contained the usual minor gauges; the righthand dial was reserved for either a vacuum gauge or (when ordered with V-8) a tachometer.

The '65s started off with the same engine lineup as

1963–64. In mid-year, however, a larger (250-cid, 150-bhp) six, a more powerful (220-bhp) 283 V-8, and a new 396-cid V-8 arrived. The 396, designed with performance in mind, was descended from the stillborn Z-11 Mark II of 1963. It was offered in either 325-bhp tune or with the now-famous "porcupine" heads (canted rocker studs, actually) and 435 bhp. The 396 was produced to help pare down the engine lineup, which had been growing wildly of late. The 426-bhp version directly replaced the 409s, while the mildly tuned 325-bhp unit largely took over for the small-block 327s (which remained theoretically

A record 243,114 SS cars were built for '65.

"Coke bottle" rear fenders marked all-new '65 styling.

available). Actually, the 396 had gobs of room left for expansion—at least 50 cubic inches more—but GM policy at the time limited all Chevrolets except Corvettes to a 400-cid maximum.

It has been suggested that the 396 was introduced because its displacement handily coincided with a proposed NASCAR racing limit (6.5 liters). That is wrong on two counts. For one thing, GM management had set the 400-cid limit arbitrarily. There was little concern with NASCAR by mid-1965, because the safety craze was on, and the last thing the company wanted was a highly visible racing program. That was the second thing: there wasn't one. The big SS competed only sporadically, did best (every so often) at the drags, and was an also-ran on the stock-car circuit. It remained what it had always been: something very special and very fast for the street.

Like other full-size Chevys, the 1966 Super Sport was a facelifted '65 with a simpler grille and less fussy ornamentation. The main changes occurred inside. The standard dash-mounted minor gauges were dropped; optional dials were available, but were relegated to the center console where you didn't have to look at them—nor could you in a hurry. The tachometer was also made optional. A 427-cid V-8 with 390 or 425 bhp joined the engine roster, relieving the high-performance 396. SS sales were far down as only 119,300 cars found homes. Interest in full-size muscle cars had peaked, and the Impala SS would be only a shadow of its former self from here on.

The SS remained a separate model for 1967, but only 76,000 were built. By and large, it resembled the other big Chevys quite closely. Gone were its individual wheel covers, unique interior, and fire-breathing big-block V-8s—the 425-bhp 427 was scratched, and the 390-bhp version detuned to 385. Only small SS medallions and a blacked-out grille provided external indentification.

Impala like this '65 was too big for the drags, but did win occasionally.

1966 Impala SS Sport Coupe

Turbo-Jet 427 with 3x2 carbs and 425 bhp

For 1968, the SS was demoted from full-fleged model to a Regular Production Option (RPO) available on any Impala two-door. At least a wide range of engine choices remained. The option's last year was 1969 when only the 427 was offered, though it was uprated back to 390 gross horsepower. SS regalia included a "427" deck emblem and G70 wide-tread red-stripe tires mounted on 15-inch wheels.

The Impala SS died for the most obvious of reasons. Market factors and the snowball effect of government regulations in the late '60s had convinced Chevrolet that it made far more sense to offer a Cadillac-style luxury car like the Caprice than a Cadillac-size street stocker like the SS. By this time, too, the "hard-core" enthusiast crowd had begun to turn to ponycars, and Chevrolet had a solid contender for that group in the Camaro. A full-size car that could do the things an SS could do had become an anachronism. What's more, it seemed very likely that the SS brand of horsepower was going to be banned by Washington in the years ahead. Ironically, there never was a law specifically barring such cars, but a changing market and rising prices made the Division's decision to drop the Impala SS inevitable. And it proved a wise one, which is hardly surprising—Chevrolet has made precious few wrong decisions in its nearly 75-year history.

Nevertheless, the Impala SS must be considered a success. It proved that the big-engine/bucket-seats-and-console formula worked as well in a big "family" car as it did in a sporty compact. In that respect, it was commercially important in paving the way for Super Sport versions of the intermediate Chevelle and the compact Chevy II. Perhaps more significant, it proved that a spacious and solid full-size machine could have astounding pickup, yet still be civilized enough for the most confirmed of big-car buyers. For luxury to go, the Impala SS was hard to beat. And come to think of it, nobody ever really did.

Clean but mean: the 1967 Impala SS Sport Coupe

1967 Impala SS convertible

Last year for SS as a separate model was 1967. SS427s numbered 2124 that year.

1964-70 Chevelle SS/SS396:

The Muscular Mid-Size

To many auto industry observers in the early '60s, it looked as if Chevrolet had missed the boat—twice. Falcon had demolished Corvair in the early compact-car battles, so the Chevy II was hurriedly launched as a stopgap. But this arrived in 1962, just as Ford trotted out something called an "intermediate" with an outstanding small-block 260 V-8. The Fairlane won sales for Ford for two years before the Chevelle arrived to counter it. In early 1964, Ford was yet another jump ahead with the Mustang. The products of this period marked the height of Ford's postwar resurgence, and it would be the last time Dearborn would seriously challenge GM's market supremacy. In the years since, General Motors (and Chevy in particular) has captured the initiative in virtually every sector. Late though it was, the Chevelle was an important part of GM's recovery.

In appearance, the new 1964 Chevelle was smoother, sleeker, and better-looking than the Fairlane. It offered a fine array of engines to suit most any need: a pair of sixes plus the well-established 283 V-8. Chevelle outsold Fairlane by a 3 to 2 margin in 1964, and no less than 67,100 of them were the memorable Malibu SS.

Writer Terry Boyce in his book, *Chevy Super Sports,* zeroed in on a big reason for the success of the Chevelle SS: it was almost a reincarnation of the great

1955–57 Chevys. "It seemed as though Chevrolet's engineers had gathered around a table [to build] a new version of the '55–'57 Bel Air. . . . The new car would incorporate the 1955–57's comparatively compact dimensions, but would also include the latest performance-type options, such as four-speed manual transmissions, engine gauges, and bucket seats, which were being installed as aftermarket items on thousands of earlier Chevrolets. Under the hood would be young America's most acclaimed engine, the

Unlike its smaller Chevy II brother, Chevelle offered a Super Sport in its first year. Shown is the '64 convertible.

First 1964 Chevelle recalled 1955-57 Chevy in size, styling, and power.

Chevrolet Turbo-Fire 283 V-8. Just for old time's sake, the optional four-barrel dual-exhaust version would be rated at 220 hp—exactly the rating known to one and all as 1957's famous 'Power Pack' 283. Even the styling would be reminiscent of the 1955 Chevy—crisp and rectangular and clean."

Although Chevelle was touted as an entirely new brand of Chevy, it was really a grown-up compact. Its basic shell was shared with the A-body Oldsmobile F-85, Pontiac Tempest, and Buick Skylark, GM's

"second-wave" compacts that were enlarged that year from their original 1961 size, which was comparable to the Chevy II. (The latter remained in the lineup, and continued to battle with Falcon.) It was a canny decision, this new car, because it was right on the money for the 1964 marketplace. The public had wearied of compacts, and many compact owners were trading up to larger—if not quite "standard size"—cars.

The Malibu SS borrowed much from the Impala SS

SS equipment was available only with the top-line Malibu trim in Chevelle's early years.

formula. There were four basic models (two-door hardtop and convertible with a choice of either six or V-8) and the same sort of standard equipment, such as vinyl bucket-seat interior, full carpeting, and a center shift console for the optional four-speed manual or Powerglide automatic. Unlike that year's Impala SS, the Malibu Super Sport was also delivered with full instrumentation as standard. A combination water temperature/amp/fuel level/oil pressure dial was slotted in the fuel/temp/warning light hole of lesser models, and an optional tachometer was placed not on the steering column, but in the spot normally occupied by an optional clock. If you ordered the tach, the clock was relocated atop the dashboard in a special mounting.

The mechanical spec for the SS was carefully chosen to exploit the Malibu's high-performance possibilities. Tires were 6.50 × 14s, and wheels were decorated with Impala SS-style wheel covers. If you didn't like the base 120-horsepower six, there was a 155-bhp version of the Chevy 230 available, but most enthusiasts specified the 283 V-8.

A 220-bhp Chevelle with the optional M-20 four-speed gearbox was not the stormer an Impala SS was, for obvious reasons. Still, you could hardly call it slow. *Motor Trend* magazine's test of such a car yielded

0–60 mph in 9.7 seconds and a quarter-mile time of 17.5 seconds at 80 mph. Later, to keep pace in performance against the likes of Pontiac GTOs and Olds Cutlass 4-4-2s, Chevrolet offered the 327 V-8 in 250- and 300-bhp tune. Engineers even tested a 365-bhp version, which naturally provided stunning performance in the lightweight Chevelle.

The 1965 model year saw only mild modifications to the Chevelle's debut-year styling, and were probably an improvement in the eyes of many. Side trim was reshuffled, and the grille cleaned up. Super Sport models had prominent SS emblems and a blacked-out grille background. Spinner wheel covers and larger 6.95 × 14 tires were also standard. A 350-bhp 327 V-8 was added to the engine lineup, but late in the model year, the first of the SS396 Chevelles arrived, boasting 375 horsepower. Production was limited to a mere 201 units, but those that survive today are among the most desirable of Super Sport Chevys. They were easily identified by their blacked-out rear panel "coves." The RPO number for the 396 package was Z-16, and brought with it dummy "mag" wheels shod with 7.75 × 14 Firestone gold-stripe tires, plus special identification.

The late-1965 model year introduction of the SS396 was largely a test of acceptance, with the prospect that

1965 Chevelle Malibu SS hardtop

Early factory photo of '65 SS396

1965 Malibu SS retained clean flanks, got new grille. SS396 arrived late that year.

every 1966 Malibu SS would be a 396. That's what happened, and except for the Chevelle-based El Camino Custom car/truck, the SS was the only model offered with the big-block engine. The '66 package was not merely an engine swap with an inadequate chassis. It also featured stiffer shocks, stronger springs, heavy-duty ball joint front suspension, and a reinforced front frame. A thick anti-sway bar and red-stripe 7.75 × 14 tires on wide rims were also added. Even with these uprated components, no SS had a base price over $3000. The hardtop was $2776, the convertible $2984. Options could, of course, raise that by another thousand or so. Buyers could choose the 360-bhp 396 instead of the standard 325-bhp unit, and 100 of the '66s were even equipped with a potent 375-bhp version.

Standardizing on the 396 did not limit the Chevelle Super Sport's appeal. Most of the SS trim items were made optional for the plain Malibu for those who thought the 396 was overkill. Thus, over 310,000 Malibus and SS396s were built. The latter did well, accounting for 72,300 units.

Few basic changes were wrought for 1967 as the Chevelle was given a minor facelift. The tachometer reverted to being a bolt-on item, and was placed too low on the steering column. However, the tach option still included a full gauge cluster, so it was possible to have a properly instrumented SS396.

New, very sleek, and aggressive-looking 112-inch wheelbase Chevelle two-doors (four-door models had a 116-inch-wheelbase chassis) debuted for 1968, the first year for significant Federal safety and emissions regulations. Performance wasn't immediately affected, and the SS396 carried on with its trio of 325/350/375-bhp big-blocks. Along with its much cleaner shape, the '68 edition featured a black-accented grille and rear deck panel, bulging hood, and black lower body finish (omitted with dark colors). It also came with F70 × 14 red-stripe tires on wide wheels, a special grille emblem, and optional SS wheel covers.

The same formula was maintained for 1969, except that the SS396 was now an option (RPO Z-25) for the Malibu hardtop and convertible, as well as the low-line 300 Deluxe hardtop and pillared coupe. The 300s were both price-competitive (about $150 less than comparable Malibus), and a bit more racing-oriented (slightly lighter and easier to "prodify"). Unfortunately, the lack of a serious racing program hampered the mid-size SS as much as it had the Impala SS, though some dragsters raced Chevelles successfully. But making the SS396 an option didn't hurt sales. Chevrolet sold 86,307 of the Z-25 packages for the model year.

The last hurrah for Chevelle performance was 1970. That was when GM finally scrapped its 400-cid maximum displacement rule for intermediates, and offered the SS equipment with a mighty 454 V-8 (bore and stroke 4.25 × 4.00) based on the Mark IV block. The SS396 model was retained, though the

All Chevelle SS models became SS396s for 1966.

Curtis Turner at Daytona in '66 Chevelle stocker

Like other Chevelles, SS396 was facelifted for 1967.

1968 SS396 packed as much as 375 bhp.

SS396s had new 112-inch wheelbase for 1968.

SS396 production peaked for '69 at 86,307.

Mighty 454 V-8 was new Chevelle SS option for 1970.

Big-inch 1970 models featured cowl-induction hood.

Power was down for 1971, but not the excitement.

1971 Chevelle SS454. Big V-8 lasted through 1975.

designation was no longer accurate as the engine had been enlarged to 402 cubes.

Recognized even in its day as the end of an era, the SS454 was far and away the fastest Chevelle ever offered, and quite possibly the hottest Chevy passenger car—period. *Hot Rod* magazine, testing a showroom-stock example, turned the quarter mile in an unbelievable 13.44 seconds, the car doing over 108 mph as it powered through the traps. The 1970 Chevelles were also beautifully styled. The cockpit bore a Monte Carlo look, with a bank of round instruments grouped within easy view of the driver. The coupe's lines were semi-fastback, with a prominent, blacked-out grille, broad racing stripes and hood bulge, bold five-spoke chrome wheels, and prominent "SS" badges front and rear. Chevelle convertibles were becoming quite rare by this time, and there would be no more after 1972.

The Chevelle SS was going out in style. The market for hot intermediates, contrary to what a lot of people say now, was still fair in 1970. But increasingly stringent Federal vehicle standards were conspiring to do in the muscle car. The choice of big- and small-blocks lasted for another year, though the 400 gave way to a 350 for 1971. Horsepower (now quoted in SAE net figures) was 245 and 270 (two- and four-barrel) for the 350, 365 and 425 for the 454. To meet emissions standards, the cars were detuned. The hottest SS454 had 11.25:1 compression in 1970, while its 1971 successor had only a 9:1 squeeze. The age of low compression and low-lead fuel was beginning, and the smooth-looking '71 was just not quite as hairy as the brilliant, powerful '70.

And so it went through the end of Chevelle SS production in 1973. An array of modest powerplants was fielded for '72, starting with a 307 V-8 (130 bhp net), and the 400-cid extension of the small-block temporarily returned to the option list. For 1973, the SS was downgraded to just a 350 in two states of tune and a single 454 with 245 bhp net. That's what it had come to. And with the convertible now a thing of the past, you could get the SS treatment only on the Malibu "Colonnade" two-door hardtop or . . . the station wagon.

In later years, the SS was effectively replaced as the sporty model in the Chevelle line by the Laguna Type S-3. This had the looks, if not always the muscle, of the SS, and the slope-nose 1975–76 version did prove popular as a NASCAR stocker. And interestingly, the big 454 V-8 was listed as a Chevelle option through 1975, though it had lost a good deal of its punch by then. Also little known is the fact that SS trim remained available for the sporty El Camino pickup right into the '80s. With this model, at least, those who wanted to remember the past were able to indulge a little.

While it lasted, the Chevelle Super Sport was one of the truly great performance cars from Chevrolet. And with the many fans who remain faithful to it to this day, you could say it still is.

1963-70 Nova SS:

Return of the Small-Block Stormer

First Nova SS was the 1963 model, but V-8 power was a year off.

A performance version of the little Chevy II compact, later known as the Nova, was the second Super Sport Chevy to appear, and lasted by far the longest. It arrived as an over-the-counter item in 1963, the second year of Chevy II production, and was still around (barely) in 1976. The reason is that it was easier for the Division to keep a smallish SS in the line, given Federal fuel economy and emissions standards, than a big-block Impala or Chevelle. But the first Nova SS did not pack a V-8. Instead, it used the 194 cubic-inch six, the top engine for the Chevy II at that time. But it did have all the equipment popularized by the big Impala SS, such as bucket seats, full carpeting, special wheel covers, and SS identification.

Chevrolet dealers were installing 327-cid Corvette V-8s in Chevy IIs as early as 1962, but the cost of the finished car was upwards of $3500—quite a lot of money back then. Mid-way through the 1963 season, the factory issued a kit for dealer installation to convert the car to 283 or 327 V-8 power. Chevy then made a 195-horsepower rendition of the 283 a factory option for 1964, which kept the price of a Nova SS hardtop to well under $3000. Obviously, it pays to have the factory in your corner! The only problem was that the '64 SS didn't arrive until spring, although the V-8 option had been listed at the start of the model year the previous autumn. Also, the Chevy II convertible was dropped that year, which meant that the SS/V-8 combo never appeared officially in a Nova ragtop.

The 195-bhp version of Chevy's reliable 283 gave the little car excellent flexibility, and together with standard HD suspension and oversize brakes plus

optional four-speed manual gearbox made the SS more than a match for certain popular sports cars. To prove this, a Nova V-8 two-door sedan driven by a Canadian dealer crossed 4000 miles of wilderness to

1963 Nova SS hardtop, shown with non-SS wheel discs.

Like all early Chevy IIs, Nova SS was clean but boxy.

All 1963 Nova SS cars had sixes. 42,342 were built.

Besides hardtop, a convertible Nova SS was listed for '63.

1965 Chevy II Nova SS hardtop.

A 1964 Nova SS lights up on a quarter-mile run.

1965 Nova SS was offered with 327 V-8.

win the Shell 4000 Rally, besting all the imported sports machines from Alfa to Triumph.

For 1965, the Nova SS continued in its basic "1964½" form. The car never sold particularly well, however, possibly because of close price and size competition from the more impressive Chevelle Super Sport. The Nova soon became a lot quicker, because during the year Chevrolet finally offered its 327, with ratings of 250 and 300 bhp. Such Novas could really fly, and the engine was light enough that it didn't have a negative effect on handling.

The Chevy II was reskinned for 1966. New, less angular tinware was applied to the 1962–65 bodyshell, so there was little change in basic dimensions— wheelbase remained at 110 inches, for instance. Engine offerings were shuffled around. You could again buy a six-cylinder SS, but you could also opt for a 275-bhp 327 V-8 or the even hairier L-79 Corvette engine with 350 horsepower. The latter delivered a 15-second quarter mile at 95 mph with the stock 3.31 rear axle ratio. This power option was, alas, dropped for 1967. It had too few buyers, and was probably

Chevy II convertibles were discontinued for '64, so only hardtops officially had V-8s. Shown is the 1965 SS327.

1966 Chevy II Nova SS hardtop

New sheetmetal for '66 made Nova SS less angular.

Chevy II V-8s (1966 shown) were popular at the drags.

1967 Chevy II Nova SS hardtop. Just 10,000 were made.

more than most customers needed. On the plus side, 1967 saw the arrival of optional front disc brakes, which really helped haul down these powerful little screamers.

Only 10,100 copies of the '67 Nova SS were built, making this model (especially in V-8 form) fairly rare, and a car to look for today. The Chevy II was about to get its third and final body/chassis change—the new 111-inch-wheelbase "X-car" that would carry on through 1979, after which it was replaced by the smaller front-wheel-drive Citation.

Because it had been engineered alongside the Camaro ponycar (which appeared a year earlier), the '68 Chevy II shared some of the same powertrains. One of these was the smooth and powerful 295-bhp V-8 from the Camaro SS350. Another, for the even more determined, was the monster 396 engine with up to 375 bhp, priced at $500. The '68 engine lineup (with the 396 increasing to 402 cid for 1970) lasted three years. The V-8s made the dowdy-looking Nova (the Chevy II handle was deleted after '68) quite a stormer. It was an ideal car for drag racing, because

Nova SS production for 1967 dropped by half from 1966. Competition from the new Camaro was a likely factor.

1968 Nova SS was all-new, offered up to 375 bhp.

virtually nothing could touch its combination of cubic inches and lightness, except a 427 Camaro.

Chevrolet sold nearly 20,000 Nova Super Sports in 1970. There were still several good years to come, but 1971 wasn't one of them. Sales were down in the industry generally, and sales of "performance cars" were down more than most. That year's Nova SS appeared with its usual identifying features—black-accented grille, simulated air intakes on front fenders, black-ribbed rear panel, and wide E70 × 15 white-stripe wires on extra-wide rims. But engine choices had been reduced to one: a detuned 350 producing just 270 net horsepower due to its lower 8.5:1 compression. A similar package returned for '72, when sales picked up slightly.

Miraculously, the Nova SS had its best year in a decade for 1973, as sales topped 35,000. Exactly what made it so popular is unclear, but a wider variety of engines must have helped. The SS could now be had with either the 350 V-8 or the new 307. Gas misers could opt for the economical 250-cid six with 100 bhp net. The SS option (RPO Z-26) now mainly involved exterior trim: black or white body striping, black-accented grille and rear panel, 14 × 6 "Rally" wheels,

Last of the truly hot Novas appeared for 1970.

'71 Rally Nova predicted the future: power was way down.

SS emblems, bright windshield and roof moldings, and sport mirrors. To this RPO you could add "Strato" bucket seats, floor console, and even genuine engine gauges and a tachometer. Considering all that had been done to emasculate it, the 175-bhp version of the 350 still made the Nova a good performer, with 0–60 mph available in under 10 seconds. Its quarter mile came up in 16–17 seconds at 85–90 mph, but a 396 it wasn't.

Undoubtedly, the Nova SS would have been axed after 1973, along with the SS Chevelle, except for its unexpectedly enthusiastic reception. So, Chevy geared up to produce it for a few more years. About 22,000 were sold for 1974, when buyers could again combine the Z-26 option with any Nova engine. The same powertrains carried on into 1975, though the poor 350 was again detuned, down to 155 net horsepower.

The 1975–76 Nova SS was, if nothing else, good-looking. The bodyshell was all-new and more European than the previous "coke-bottle" look. Special paint jobs, with black accents around the window area, plus slot-style wheels and clean front and rear styling concealed a thoroughly revised chassis that borrowed heavily from the second-series Camaro. The practical hatchback coupe body style first seen in '73 was continued, along with the "trunked" coupe and four-door sedan. But only about 9000 of the '75s and just 3000 of the '76s were sold with the SS option before it was finally dropped from the books. Towards the end, it seemed that it was just being kept around for sentiment's sake.

SS specialist Terry Boyce says that "only the 396-engined 1968–70 versions of the last type of Novas are avidly sought by collectors. But then, there was a time when no one wanted a 1957 Chevy as a collector car, either." If the Chevy II and Nova Super Sports do achieve broad collector appeal, it would be no more surprising than what happened with the "classic" 1955–57 Chevys. When you come right down to it, these cars had something for every sort of performance fan. They were the right size, and with their light weight, a big-block engine made them sheer dynamite. If you're not the drag-race type, you'll find an SS327 makes a fine road car.

You could even get a decent Nova *after* 1976. The SS was succeeded by the Rally Nova, and things like buckets, gauges, four-speeds, and 350s stayed on the option list. In 1979, a colleague of ours bought one of the last coupes with the Rally Nova package, which included HD suspension, extra instruments, sport striping, and slot wheels. He paid a pittance for it, because the Nova was about to go out of production, and the dealer was anxious to get rid of it. What he got was the performance and finesse of a mid-range imported sports sedan. The only thing he regrets now is that it doesn't get 35 miles per gallon. But that isn't much to moan about in a car that cost around $4500 new and can do just about everything an $8000 import can.

Above: 1964 Impala SS   Below: 1964 Chevelle Malibu SS

Above: 1965 Chevy II Nova SS   Below: 1966 Impala SS

Above: 1965 Corvair Corsa (pre-production)   Inset and Below: 1966 Chevy II Nova SS

Above and Inset: 1967 Impala SS   Below: 1967 Chevelle SS396

Above and Inset: 1968 Chevelle SS396   Below: 1968 Impala SS

Above and Upper Inset: 1969 Camaro Z-28   Below and Lower Inset: 1968 Corvette 427

Above: 1969 Corvette Stingray 454   Below: 1969 Chevelle SS396

Above and Inset: 1969 Camaro Z-28 (modified)   Below: 1970 Chevelle SS396

1963-67 Corvette Sting Ray:

Excitement and Excellence

Bill Mitchell's Stingray racer was campaigned with modest success in 1960 by Dr. Dick Thompson.

Of all Corvettes, the 1963–67 Sting Ray has come to be regarded as the greatest in history. There is a remarkable new Corvette coming for 1983, but it will have to go a long way to supplant the Sting Ray in the affection of enthusiasts.

The engineering brief for 1963, according to Corvette "father" Zora Arkus-Duntov, was "better driver and passenger accommodation, better luggage space, better ride, better handling, and higher performance." Styling Staff's contribution to these goals began in late 1959 with project XP-720 based on the racing Stingray (spelled as one word here and on production models after 1967). Besides the traditional roadster, a new closed coupe was planned, for which Bill Mitchell had conceived the unusual split rear window. The result was practical as well as

aggressively handsome. Hidden headlights mounted on pivoting sections that fit flush with and matched the front-end contour, a dipped beltline, and doors cut into the coupe's roof were among the Sting Ray's novel styling features. The twin-cockpit dashboard design, which had been present in one form or another since the 1953 Corvette, was retained. "It was a very fresh approach to two-passenger styling, and I think it worked remarkably well," said one GM designer.

Ed Cole had wanted a four-passenger version as well, but both Mitchell and Duntov fought this, saying the car's distinction and personality would be compromised. A 2+2 coupe was also considered and discarded.

The production-ready '63 coupe and roadster were tested intensively, including wind tunnel evaluations at

Stingray racer was financed out of Mitchell's own pocket.

After its racing career, Stingray got Corvette badges.

Top power for '63 Sting Ray was 360-bhp "fuelie" 327.

Split-window Sting Ray coupe was limited to 1963.

A modern classic: the 1963 Corvette Sting Ray coupe

Cal Tech. Body engineers spent a great deal of effort revising the car's inner structure. Compared to the '62 Corvette, the Sting Ray had nearly twice as much steel support built into its central body structure. But this was balanced by a reduction in fiberglass content, so the finished car actually weighed less than a '62. Wheelbase was shortened from 102 to 98 inches, the rear track was made two inches narrower, and frontal area was reduced by a square foot. Yet interior space was as good as before, and, thanks to the added steel reinforcement, the cockpit was both stronger and safer. Other body features included curved door glass, cowl-top ventilation, increased luggage space, and an improved fresh-air heater. Neither coupe nor roadster had an external trunklid as in '62. This meant you had to pull the seatbacks down for access to the luggage space. The spare tire resided in an external hinged compartment that dropped down to ground level for access.

Engines were carried over from 1962, but the brand-new body was matched by a modified chassis, with most of the changes at the back. For the first time, a Corvette had independent rear suspension—a three-link type, with double-jointed open driveshafts on each side, plus control arms and trailing radius rods. A single transverse leaf spring (there was no room for coils) was mounted to the frame with rubber-cushioned struts, and the differential was bolted to the rear crossmember. The frame itself was a well-reinforced box shape. Front/rear weight distribution was improved to 48/52 from the previous 53/47. As a result of all this, ride and handling were much better, and axle tramp was virtually absent. A new recirculating-ball steering gear and three-link ball-joint front suspension gave fewer turns lock-to-lock than before, and the front brake drums were wider. An alternator replaced the generator, positive crankcase ventilation was fitted, the clutch housing was now aluminum, and the flywheel was smaller than before.

Competition options were mainly designed with the new coupe in mind. They included heavy-duty springs and shocks, a stiffer anti-sway bar, metallic brake linings, optional Al-Fin aluminum brake drums, cast-aluminum knock-off wheels, dual master cylinder, and a 36.5-gallon fuel tank. Full leather upholstery became an interior option.

Road testers raved about the new, exotic-looking Sting Ray, and special comments were made on its improved traction. The new car neither hopped during hard acceleration nor oversteered on tight bends. In driving the coupe through hard S-turns, *Road & Track* magazine reported: "Every time through we discovered we could have gone a little faster. We never did find the limit."

The excitement generated by the Sting Ray during its brief production life stemmed partly from its steady improvement each year. Contrary to the old Detroit axiom that you must add more trim and decoration on each succeeding model, Chevy actually removed the

Cast aluminum wheels were a new option for '63.

1963 Sting Ray roadsters with and without hardtop

1964 Corvette Sting Ray coupe

stuff. In 1964, for example, the controversial split rear window disappeared, much to Mitchell's chagrin. Though it added "character," it also reduced rear visibility. Also erased for '64 were the fake louvers on the hood. Slotted wheel discs were added, and the '63's dummy roof vents were made functional to serve as interior air extractors. For 1965, the hood panel was

planed smooth, and the front fender slots were opened up to duct heat out of the engine compartment. The relatively inefficient extractor vents were deleted for 1966, when an eggcrate grille was adopted. For 1967, its fourth and final year, the Sting Ray reached near design perfection. The only styling changes this time were an oblong backup light, revised front fender

Absence of dummy hood vents and new one-piece rear window marked the 1964 Sting Ray.

Last year for fuel injection was 1965 when the Sting Ray 327 churned out up to 375 bhp.

1966 Sting Ray roadster with 427 Turbo-Jet V-8

Big-engined Corvettes were nothing new, of course. Mickey Thompson's specials for Daytona and other races had appeared with the 409 engine as early as 1962. Zora Arkus-Duntov had at first resisted the idea of a big-block option, but by '64 the need was apparent. Cars like the Shelby Cobra were not outselling the Corvette, but they were trouncing it in competition. Duntov teamed with Jim Premo, who had replaced Harry Barr as Chevrolet chief engineer, to work out the adaptation.

The first Mark IV displaced 396 cubic inches (4.09 × 3.75), mainly because GM policy in those days restricted cars of intermediate size and smaller to engines of less than 400 cid. For Corvette, the 396 replaced the small-block (365-bhp) option. It packed 425 bhp at 6400 rpm and 415 lbs-ft of torque at 4000 rpm, thanks to 11:1 compression, solid lifters, and four-barrel carburetor. To handle this brute force, engineers added stiffer front springs, a thick front anti-sway bar, a new rear bar, a heavier clutch, and a larger radiator and fan. Though the Mark IV engine weighed over 650 pounds, it did not adversely affect weight distribution, which remained near neutral at 51/49 front/rear. An aggressive-looking hood bulge and optional side-mounted exhaust pipes completed an impressive package.

For 1966, a bore increase to 4.25 inches gave 427

louvers, bolt-on instead of knock-off aluminum wheels, and an optional black vinyl covering for the roadster's removable hardtop.

Mechanically, however, each of these years brought important advancements. The new fuel-injected 375-bhp small-block 1964 engine developed 1.15 bhp per cubic inch, and could propel the 'Vette from 0 to 100 mph in 15 seconds flat. For 1965, four-wheel disc brakes were offered optionally, something enthusiasts had long been demanding, and made for awesome braking power. Also that year came another big step forward in performance: the Mark IV V-8.

More Sting Rays were made for 1966 than any other year.

The last was the best: the 1967 Sting Ray coupe

Sting Ray had the briefest production run of any Corvette. Revised fender gills mark this as a '67.

cubic inches—and truly stupendous acceleration. With a car pulling the short 4.11:1 gearset, *Sports Car Graphic* magazine managed 0–60 mph in a nearly unbelievable 4.8 seconds, 0–100 in 11.2 seconds, and a maximum of 140 mph. The only car that could keep up with this Corvette was the 427 Cobra—and that was far less refined, with few of the high-speed comfort qualities of the Sting Ray. Though the 427 Cobra was a formidable competitor on the track, the big-inch Mark IV Corvette was really in a class by itself everywhere else.

Other engine happenings during the 1963–67 period bear mentioning. Fuel injection was dropped after 1965, mainly due to high production cost, low sales, and the advent of the Mark IV program. Engine options by years are as follows:

Years	bhp/rpm	cid/induction
1963–65	250/4400	327/carb
1963–67	300/5000	327/carb
1963	340/6000	327/carb
1965–67	350/5800	327/carb
1963	360/6000	327/FI
1964–65	375/6200	327/FI
1965	425/6400	396/carb
1966–67	390/5400	427/carb

Years	bhp/rpm	cid/induction
1964–65	365/6200	327/carb
1966–67	350/5800	327/carb
1966	425/6400	427/carb
1967	400/5400	427/carb
1967	435/5800	427/carb

By the time Elliott M. "Pete" Estes had relieved Semon E. "Bunkie" Knudsen as Chevrolet general manager in 1965, the Corvette was permanently established in the divisional picture, with 20,000-plus sales a year. The production figures for each model year of the Sting Ray generation indicate strong and steady success:

Year	Coupe	Conv.	Total
1963	10,594	10,919	21,513
1964	8,304	13,925	22,229
1965	8,186	15,376	23,562
1966	9,958	17,762	27,720
1967	8,504	14,436	22,940

By now the AMA's anti-performance resolution was ancient history, and Chevrolet set about preparing a competition reply to the big-block Cobra. Their answer

Sting Ray was always a hot contender on the dragstrips, as this much-modified '66 shows.

Bob Johnson's 1966 A-production coupe powers through a turn at Mid-Ohio.

was the Grand Sport, with a special 377-cid aluminum V-8. Only five were built, forcing it to compete in SCCA class C-Modified. At Daytona 1963, all three Grand Sports were 10 seconds a lap faster than the Cobras. Roger Penske won at Nassau that year, and Grand Sports were still racing as late as 1966, though by then they had been outclassed. Their problem was not so much performance as it was numbers. Had Chevrolet been willing to produce the minimum 100 cars necessary to qualify for a production class, the Grand Sport would have been unstoppable in the mid-'60s.

For 1966, Arkus-Duntov introduced his L-88 engine option on the 427 block—560 horsepower, the most powerful engine ever available for a Corvette. It sat in a chassis featuring the now-famous F-41 suspension package, heavy-duty brakes and Positraction. Unfortunately, the production Corvette just wasn't competitive with the 427 Cobra in SCCA's class A-production. The Cobra had almost as much horsepower, and was lighter by half a ton.

There *was* a place, however, for the big, strong, heavy Corvettes—endurance racing. In 1966, for example, Penske's team finished 12th overall and first in the GT class at the Daytona Continental. They were also ninth overall at Sebring, and again first in class. The next year, Dave Morgan and Don Yenko placed tenth overall and first in GT at Sebring. Bob Bondurant

and Dick Guildstrand actually led the highly competitive GT class at Le Mans for several hours until their engine blew sky high. Endurance racing held great promise for the big-block Corvettes, but their potential wasn't adequately exploited.

By this time, Chevrolet was committed to providing underground support to Can-Am racers like Jim Hall and Trans-Am Camaro teams like Penske's. In effect, Chevy had abandoned the sports-car classes to Shelby's Cobras, and went to play on a different field where it had a better chance of winning. Given the restrictions of the GM bureaucracy, it was impossible for Chevy to work with an outside subcontractor the way Ford did with Carroll Shelby. It was equally impossible to turn a mass-production sports car like the Corvette into an unqualified champion against hand-built machines created strictly for racing. Chevy was forced literally to wait out Henry Ford II's interest in competition. The Cobras were happily allowed to die in December 1967 in the face of forthcoming Federal emissions and safety regulations. At that point, the Corvette's competition prospects improved greatly.

What was undeniable, though, was that the Sting Ray provided some of the most exciting motoring ever offered Americans. It was fast, very capable on any kind of road, and wonderful to look at. It's no wonder so many have been preserved today.

Another Sting Ray rival in the '60s was the Shelby-Mustang GT-350, shown here at Mid-Ohio in 1966.

Don Yenko's 427 Sting Ray leads Ed Lowther's Cobra 427 at Mid-Ohio, June 1966.

Two A-production Sting Ray coupes, '65 (left) and '66 (right) in SCCA National competition at Mid-Ohio

1968-71 Corvette:

The Last Word in Performance

1968 Corvette roadster with 427 V-8

The Europeans have a "thing" about the post-1967 Corvette. Plainly put, they love it. It may not have any suds anymore, but they just don't care. They think it's one of the wildest-looking street sports cars ever built anywhere—by anybody. Many Americans seem to agree: they continue to buy this now-14-year-old design in enormous numbers. The fifth-generation Corvette is due to be phased out for 1983, and will probably become a hot collector's item—the last of the "big" 'Vettes. But it wasn't always the desmogged, "Naderized" car we've come to know in the last few years. It its early days, it was as mean as the meanest Sting Ray.

The beautiful 1963 Corvette was hardly on the market a year when GM Styling Staff began planning its successor. The new model might actually have been a far different, mid-engine design. In preparation for such a development, Styling Staff created a prototype with a sharply raked front end, broad expanses of curved glass, skirted rear wheels, and nothing less than a functional periscope to provide rearward visibility. But over at Engineering Staff, the high cost of the necessary transaxle condemned the mid-engine configuration to the reject pile. Accordingly, the production 'Vette emerged with a conventional mechanical layout, and bore a strong relationship to the experimental Mako Shark II.

The final styling work was directed by David Holls of the Chevrolet Studio, who couldn't have been a better choice. Holls had always been—and still is—an automobile connoisseur and an enthusiastic driver as well as a talented stylist. His personality was reflected

in the finished product. Holls kept the ground-hugging snoot of the Mako II, but notched its fastback roofline slightly and added a Kamm-style rear deck with a spoiler.

There was only one problem: air drag, which proved to be considerably greater than expected. Although the new car was supposed to be introduced as a 1967 model, Zora Arkus-Duntov convinced division general manager Elliott M. "Pete" Estes to hold it back until 1968 so wind tunnel tests could be made. These resulted in lower front fenders, a redesigned notch-back, and—a surprise—a lower rear spoiler (the initial one had actually impeded air flow). Rear glass was also altered to improve visibility, and front fender louvers were enlarged to improve cooling and reduce drag. An air dam was built into the front under-bumper pan, and headlights were hidden under panels that fit flush when closed.

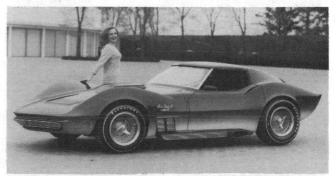

1965's Mako Shark II showcar inspired '68 Corvette.

The '68 Corvette was offered with the 1967 engine lineup, which meant you could order Duntov's mighty L-88 racing powerplant with up to 560 horsepower. It featured aluminum heads with 12.5:1 compression, oversize valves, aluminum intake manifold, and a small-diameter flywheel with beefed-up clutch. The L-88 was joined in 1969 by another racing mill, the aluminum-block ZL-1 dry-sump engine. This weighed 100 pounds less than the L-88, but was listed at an astounding $3000 on the option book. Since these engines were not really street equipment, they're not shown on the accompanying charts.

At first, the '68 Corvette was not as well-liked as it came to be later—probably because the 1963–67 design was such a hard act to follow. The new body was seven inches longer (most of it in front overhang), though wheelbase remained at 98 inches. The interior was more cramped, and there was less luggage space. Some road testers bemoaned the new car's greater weight, up by 150 pounds compared to the '67. Yet it was still so all-fired superior to almost every other Detroit car that it had no problem winning acceptance. A total of 28,566 of the '68s were sold; for 1969, that figure was shattered with 38,762 units, a record that would stand until 1976.

Zora Arkus-Duntov regained considerable influence over Corvette development in time to affect the 1969 model, which he again named "Stingray" (the name—in two-word form—was dropped on the '68s). The exterior was cleaned up. Black-painted grille bars replaced bright metal ones, and backup lights merged with the inner taillights. Wider-rim wheels improved handling, a stiffer frame decreased body shake, and somehow a bit more room was found inside. The smaller 327 engine was stroked to 350 cubic inches, and offered either 300 or 350 horsepower—"one hp per cubic inch" was now nothing unusual for a hot Chevy.

The 1969 formula was happily unchanged for the 1970 edition, although price zoomed to over $5000 base, up about $600 from the previous year. Sales were down substantially—to 17,316 units—but then 1970 was not the year 1969 had been throughout the industry.

Chevy sold 21,801 of the '71 Corvettes, and gave some of them the big 454 V-8. This was less a performance move, however, than an attempt to bring engine offerings in line with increasingly tough Federal emission mandates. It actually developed less horsepower than the 1968–69 427. A 465–bhp version of the 454 was planned, but was withdrawn due to certification problems. Meanwhile, the solid-lifter small-block, the LT-1, was producing a vigorous 370 bhp at 6000 rpm on an 11:1 compression ratio for

The shape of things to come: the 1968 Corvette. Styling has been remarkably little changed since.

1968 Corvette coupe helped popularize "targa" roof.

After a year's absence, Stingray name returned for '69.

Eggcrate grille and fender vents marked 1970 'Vette.

Corvette engines were detuned for '72 to meet emission regs.

Last year for genuine high-power 'Vettes was 1971.

Jerry Thompson's Sting Ray at Mid-Ohio, 1968

1970. Alas, this fine powerplant was also much tamed for '71, when compression sighed to 9.00:1, and output sank to a rated 330 bhp.

These were the last years for the high-compression, high-power Corvettes. The changes that occurred after 1970 are dramatic, as the following chart demonstrates (horsepower figures are SAE gross ratings):

Year	CID	bhp/rpm	C.R.
1968	327	350/5800	11.0:1
1969–70	350	300/4800	10.25:1
1969–70	350	350/5600	11.0:1
1970	350	370/6000	11.0:1
1971–72	350	270/4800	8.5:1
1971–72	350	330/5600	9.0:1
1968–69	427	400/5400	10.25:1
1968–69	427	435/5800	11.0:1
1969	427	430/5200	12.5:1
1970	454	390/4800	10.25:1
1970	454	465/5200	12.25:1
1971	454	425/5600	9.0:1
1971–72	454	365/4800	8.5:1

Thus, 1972 was a turning point—from an emphasis on horsepower and specific output to low emissions and low compression. There were no mechanical-lifter engines and no LT-1 for '73, and the 350, producing 270–330 bhp gross in 1972, was now rated at 190–250 bhp net. The only remaining Mark IV was a detuned 454 with 9.0:1 compression and 270 net horsepower, though even this was a "performer" in the context of 1973.

There's no secret about which post-1967 Corvettes are the ones to look for, whether you're a collector, a high-performance fan, or both. A generation from now,

Corvettes of the '70s will be only a fond memory, but LT-1s and 427s will have survived in high numbers. They will thus join the Sting Ray and the "fuelie" '57 among Chevy's performance greats.

Tony DeLorenzo inches past Thompson...

... to take the flag in a 1968 SCCA A-production clash.

1967-69 Camaro Z-28:

The Z Stood for "Zoom!"

Probably no other car typifies Chevrolet's devotion to high performance more than the Camaro Z-28. And no Z-28 was closer to the concept of a near-race car you could buy and use on the street than the early ones, the 1967–69 editions.

Basically the Z-28 (the designation became the most famous of Chevy Regular Production Options) was created to help capture the upper division of the SCCA's Trans-Am Championship, a racing series for stock "sedans" begun in 1966. The Camaro qualified as a sedan because it had a rear seat. SCCA said you had to build 1000 of any model to qualify it as a production car. Chevy sold only 602 Z-28s in 1967, but met the requirement by homologating the "cooking" 350-cid Camaro under FIA Group I rules, then qualifying this car with RPO Z-28 under Group II.

Engineer Vince Piggins was the Z-car's father, and had originally planned to settle for a 283 V-8 in the "factory racer." He really wanted to use the 327, but that was too large for the SCCA's 305-cid displacement limit. With approval from division chief Elliott M. "Pete" Estes, Piggins combined the 327 block with the 283's crankshaft, which yielded a 4 × 3-inch bore and stroke—exactly 302 cid.

Officially, Chevrolet listed power output at 290 bhp at 5800 rpm, but it's important to keep in mind that this was a nominal figure. Somebody just plugged it into the spec sheets, probably hoping to keep the Z-28 insurable. In reality, the 302 developed at least 350 bhp, and racing versions were tuned to produce up to 500 bhp. It all depended on intake and exhaust manifolds, carburetors, and internal modifications. But whatever the rated horsepower, all street Zs carried the same two-year/24,000-mile general warranty and five-year/50,000-mile powertrain warranty as other Chevys.

Buying a Z-28 in 1968 involved a lengthy ordering procedure. You would start with the basic six-cylinder Camaro coupe priced at $2964, add the Z-28 equipment (not available for the convertible), and go on from there. The Z-28 package comprised the 302 engine, F-41 heavy-duty suspension, Corvette "Rally" wheels, Goodyear wide-tread GT tires, special hood and deck striping, N-44 quick-ratio steering, and special 302 front fender emblems. But to get the Z-28 goodies you also had to take two "mandatory options"—front disc brakes with vacuum assist ($100) and one of three four-speed transmissions (at least $184). In all, the Z-28 added at least $700 to the price of the base Camaro coupe.

Above that was Chevrolet's long list of other Camaro options, which contained many temptations. Consider such items as the Rally Sport package ($105),

"Privateer" Z-28 in a 1968 Trans-Am race

1968 Z-28 with optional Rally Sport equipment

1969 Z-28 featured new optional cold-air hood.
Note its bold striping and "302" numerals.

fiberglass rear spoiler ($33), Positraction ($42), the even-quicker N-40 power steering option ($84), and the all-but-essential sintered metallic rear brake linings ($38). The factory would also be glad to supply a set of tuned steel headers for $200, but you'd have to pay a dealer to install them—the factory left them in the trunk. For another $500 you could have the dual Holley 600-cfm carburetors on a special manifold, and these, too, had to be dealer-installed. So it wasn't impossible to work your Z-28's window sticker up to $5000. Even that was ridiculously small change, considering what you got—by today's inflation-ridden values, it seems almost unbelievable.

Despite enthusiastic buyer reception, the Z-28 was really developed as Chevy's racing weapon against Ford. And race it did. The first 25 were built before mid-January 1967 (contrary to some reports the Z-28

was not a "1967½" introduction). Most were sent to dealerships with an active competition involvement, such as Don Yenko and Roger Penske in Pennsylvania, Nickey Chevrolet in Chicago, and Ron Tonkin in Portland, Oregon. Most of these dealers quickly began entering the cars in Trans-Am events.

In due course, the exercise paid off handsomely. Camaro won the over-2.5-liter championship in both 1968 and '69. That meant—to Chevy's unmitigated delight—that the Boss Mustang was an also-ran.

Though many driver/dealer teams fielded Z-28s, the one that stood out most was the dynamic duo of Mark Donohue and Roger Penske. Penske, a fine racing driver in his own right, had long involved his dealership in the sport, and had known Donohue since their early days in SCCA.

The engine of the Penske/Donohue car was

Racing great Jim Rathman and the '69 Indy pace car

Wild '68 SS drag car launches down the strip.

Z-28's first race wins were scored by Mark Donohue in this Roger Penske car—with much help from Chevy.

beautifully prepared by California's Traco Inc., but Donohue himself devised the chassis specs, which he admitted he didn't know much about. The car's initial race outings were plagued by inadequate braking and handling. Then Chevrolet Research and Development stepped in. Braking woes were cured by reversing the lines to allow the larger master cylinder piston to work the front discs instead of the rear drums. Then, Donohue and car were invited to GM's Milford, Michigan, proving grounds for extensive testing. The body was stiffened to prevent flex, and suspension adjustments were made. Donohue soon started winning. The Z-28's first victory came at the tight Upper Marlboro, Maryland, circuit where the car

Brutal appearance and performance: the 1969 Z-28

The '69 Z-28's dual-carb 302 and special air cleaner

averaged an astounding 63 mph. But by now it was too late in the season to accomplish much.

The 1968 Trans-Am kick-off at Daytona proved disappointing, as Camaro finished second in class. But at Sebring, the two Penske team cars placed third and fourth overall (behind Porsche 911s), and took the GT class one-two. After that, Camaro won everything in sight, capturing 9 of the 11 remaining Trans-Am races to win the over-2.5-liter championship outright. The following year, after considerable development work using computer-design techniques and a van packed with sophisticated race telemetry devices, Camaro scored eight wins in the 12-race Trans-Am schedule to capture its second straight title.

The production 1969 Z-28 was distinguished by a new "cold-air" hood featuring a rear-facing scoop angled to catch the wind at a point of maximum turbulence. The 302 V-8 was switched to four-bolt main bearings, and the 15-inch Rally wheels were slimmed down from 7 to 6 inches in width. Firestone E70-15 "Sports Car 200" tires were adopted, and four-wheel disc brakes became an RPO instead of a restricted-availability "service option." The '69 was a tremendous hit in the showrooms: 19,014 were built against only 7199 of the 1968s and 602 of the '67 models. This mark was never bettered.

How fast was a Z-28? Would you believe 174.344 mph? That was what Mickey Thompson accomplished in the flying mile at Bonneville in October 1967. Your street Z was not tuned or geared to this level, of course, but a good one would do 0–60 mph in about 5.5 seconds and a standing quarter mile in 13.75 seconds at 107 mph—those were *Car and Driver* magazine's figures. Think about it.

Few would argue that the first-generation Z-28 marked a high point in Chevrolet's high-performance history. There will never be a rip-snorting, fire-breathing, grand tourer like this again. Those that have survived have long been prized enthusiast possessions. Prettier Camaros have been made since, including the beautiful new 1982, but they'll never match the early Zs for speed and excitement—or wonderful memories.

1970-71 Monte Carlo SS454:

Discreet Dynamite

Big-engine Montes carried no special grille or identifying insignia at the front.

Now some of you have read about the Impala, Chevelle, and Nova Super Sports, and have not been moved. After all, you say, they were only sedans with big engines—not a sporty body in the lot. Well, sir, what you need is a 1970–71 Monte Carlo SS454. It's sort of a Thunderbird with teeth—an automotive "Jaws."

The Monte Carlo was designed and produced to nibble away at the "personal-luxury" field that Ford had uncovered with the Thunderbird, and that Pontiac, Buick, and Olds were happily plowing with their Grand Prix, Riviera, and Toronado, respectively. The first MC, the 1970 model, was of the close-coupled, short-deck genre—flawlessly styled, and with the longest hood ever riveted onto a Chevy. There was precious little room in the back seat, but nobody cared. Chevy sold 130,000 Montes in its first year alone.

If all this sounds like the recipe for just another boulevard barge, consider RPO Z-20, which made the Monte Carlo into a genuine red-blooded Super Sport. It gave you the big-block 454 with 360 gross

horsepower, 10.25:1 compression, and 500—count 'em—pounds-feet of torque at 3200 rpm. SS454 lettering and thin black accent stripes along the rocker panels provided subtle ID for those who knew where to look. Square dual exhaust tips poking out the back

The 1970 Monte Carlo dash, with full instrumentation.

end were what a lot of other surprised drivers mainly got to see, as this car's top speed was on the order of 135 mph. Off-the-line acceleration was vivid, to say the least: 0–60 mph in 7.7 seconds and the quarter mile in 16.2 seconds at 90-plus mph, according to *Car Life* magazine's road test—and this for a car that weighed 4000 pounds with two passengers aboard.

What you didn't see, but surely felt, was the SS454 chassis. It was beefed up with automatic level control acting on rear air shocks, stiffer front shocks, and standard power front disc brakes. For an American car in the Grand Touring tradition, look no further. And it didn't cost much over $4000 new.

As has quite often been the case with Chevy's performance cars, a handful of interesting non-standard options found their way into SS Montes. For example, there were at least 10 built with the LS-6 engine packing 450 horsepower. Some of these, and a few others besides, also had M-series four-speed

manuals, although Turbo Hydra-matic was officially listed as the standard and only transmission. Chances are there are still one or two very interesting SS Monte Carlos running around out there. All you have to do is find one—regrettably, not an easy task as only 3823 were made for 1970.

It was much the same story the following year, except that only 1919 SS454s were built . At least they had stronger identification, including SS454 nameplates on lower-fender molding inserts, black-accented rear panel with SS emblems, and 15 × 7 Rally wheels. But strangely, there was still nothing to identify them up front—and that's where everybody looks. It's quite likely that the lack of an SS-style blackout grille was a serious disadvantage. As in 1970, a few of the big-inch '71s were built with four-speeds and the LS-6 engine (now rated at 425 bhp gross). After that, the SS454 vanished, never to return.

The reasons are obvious. The muscular Monte

Monte Carlo was a solid sales hit, but not in SS form; only 3823 of the 1970 models were built.

New for 1970, Monte Carlo was based on Chevelle platform. Chevy's longest-ever hood is evident in this photo.

didn't sell because it was a contradiction in terms. The buyer who was attracted to a Toronado, T-Bird, or Riviera would never dream of stomping the local hotshoes at a downtown traffic light on a summer night after the movies let out. Of course, Monte Carlos sold and sold well—mostly to aspiring younger executives who wanted more luxury than a Chevelle without the bulk of a Caprice . . . and to banker types who were tired of Thunderbirds. Accordingly, Chevrolet deleted the Super Sport treatment from the Monte Carlo catalog. In fact, the 1972 brochure even went so far as to declare, "Sorry, no four-on-the-floor."

Nevertheless, Chevy did see a place for a sportier-than-standard model, and announced the Monte Carlo S for 1973. More grand tourer than Super Sport, it came with a tighter-than-normal suspension and blackwall radials. It sold reasonably well through 1974, when it, too, was dropped. Like the Pontiac Grand Am, it was a good idea, but wasn't the sort of thing to light

the fire of the typical personal-luxury buyer. Writer Don Vorderman said of the Grand Am, "Get one quick before they change it." He could have been talking of the Monte Carlo S as well.

"We did right in not gooking up the Monte Carlo," a Chevrolet designer told us recently. "You have to remember that all those 'graphics' on the Impala, Chevelle, and Nova had a real purpose. What they did was proclaim that this wasn't just your everyday, ordinary Chevy passenger car. But the Monte Carlo didn't need 'em. You could tell at a glance it was out of the ordinary."

Maybe so, but we have a prediction: in 10 or 15 years, the owner of a Monte Carlo SS454 will have the fastest-appreciating investment among all of Chevy's SS cars. It was that rare exception: a hot car that didn't shout "PERFORMANCE!" Discreet? Perhaps—but definitely dynamite. With that sort of power, it couldn't be anything else.

Slightly bolder ornamentation marked the 1971 SS454. Most obvious were the 15x7 Rally wheels shown.

Beefier chassis and 454 muscle made the Monte Carlo SS a capable road machine, and a rapid one.

Hi-Performance Chevrolet Model Year Production

CORVETTE

	roadster	coupe
1953	300	—
1954	3,640	—
1955	700	—
1956	3,467	—
1957	6,339	—
1958	9,168	—
1959	9,670	—
1960	10,261	—
1961	10,939	—
1962	14,531	—
1963	10,919	10,594
1964	13,925	8,304
1965	15,376	8,186
1966	17,762	9,958
1967	14,436	8,504
1968	18,630	9,936
1969	16,608	22,154
1970	6,648	10,668
1971	7,121	14,680

"GOLDEN AGE" CHEVYS

	One-Fifty	Two-Ten	Bel Air	Nomad*
1955	125,446	805,309	773,382	8,530
1956	157,294	737,371	669,281	8,103
1957	146,080	653,358	702,651	6,534

*part of total Bel Air production

CHEVROLET IMPALA*

1958	60,000	
1959	402,200	(V-8 cvt: 65,800)
1960	411,000	(V-8 cvt: 100,000)
1961	426,400	(V-8 cvt: 64,600)

*to nearest 100 units

IMPALA SUPER SPORT

1961	453	(409 V-8: 142)
1962	100,000*	(409 V-8: 15,019)
1963	153,271	
1964	185,325	
1965	243,114	
1966	119,314	
1967	76,055	(SS427: 2,124)
1968	38,210	(SS427: 1,778)
1969	2,455	(all SS427)

*estimated

CORVAIR MONZA SPYDER/CORSA

	coupe		convertible
1962	6,894		2,574
1963	11,627		7,472
1964	6,480		4,761
1965*	20,291	(total turbos: 7,206)	8,353
1966*	7,330	(total turbos: 1,951)	3,142

*includes non-turbocharged models

CHEVELLE SUPER SPORT/SS396

1964	76,860	
1965	101,577	(SS396: 201)
1966	72,300	(all SS396)
1967	63,000	(all SS396)
1968	62,785	(all SS396)
1969	86,307	(all SS 396)
1970	53,599	(454 V-8: 3,733)
1971	80,000*	(454 V-8: 19,292)
1972	24,946	(454 V-8: 3,000)
1973	28,647	(454 V-8: 2,500*)

*estimated

CHEVY II/NOVA SUPER SPORT

1963	42,432	(6-cylinder only)
1964	10,576	
1965	9,100	
1966	21,000	
1967	10,100	
1968	5,571	(incl. 667 w/L-78 V-8)
1969	17,564	(SS396: 7,209)
1970	19,558	
1971	7,015	
1972	12,309	
1973	35,542	
1974	21,419	
1975	9,067	
1976	3,000*	

*estimated

MONTE CARLO SS454

1970	3,823
1971	1,919

CAMARO Z-28

1967	602
1968	7,199
1969	19,014